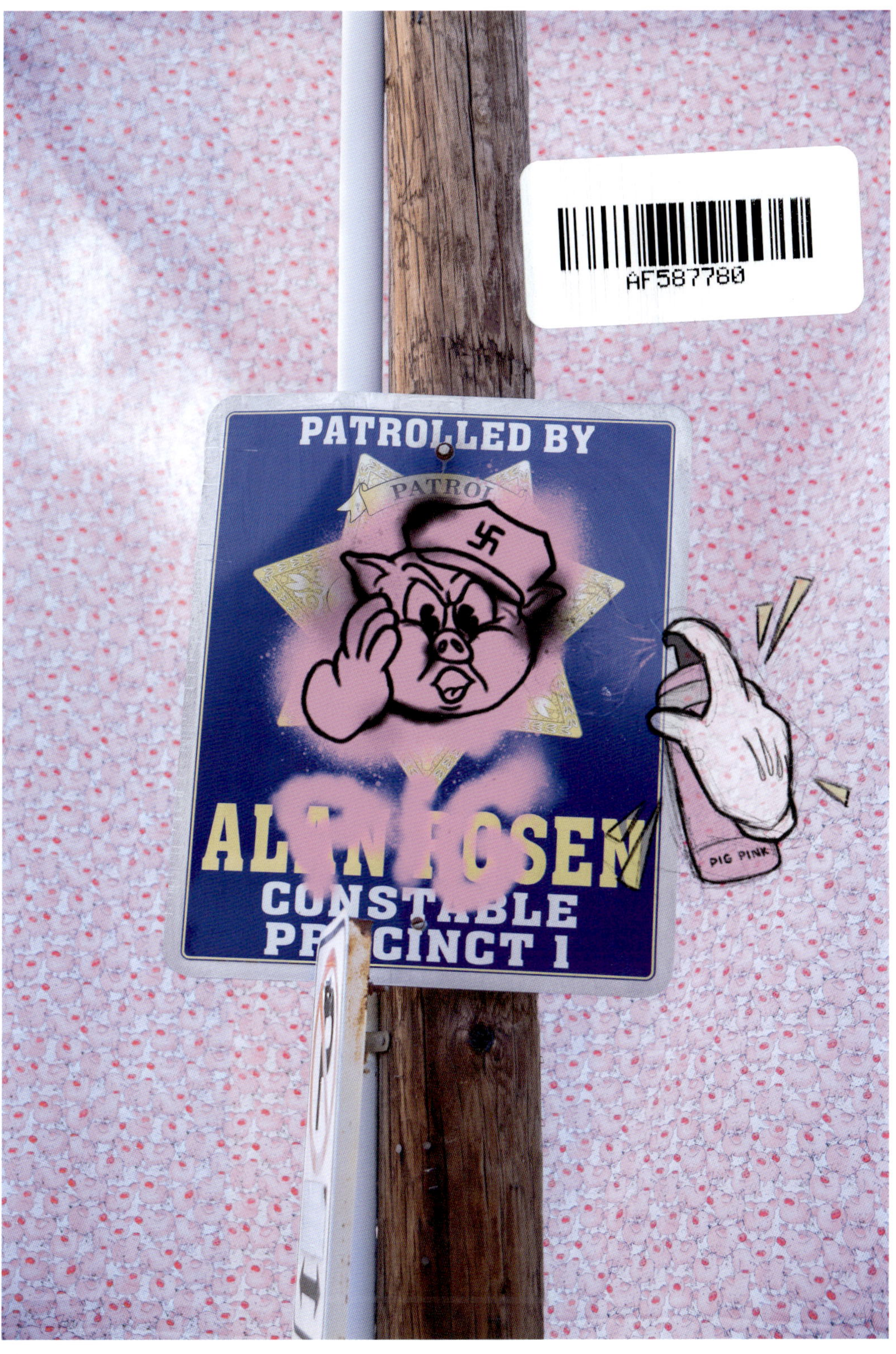
PATROLLED BY
PATROL
PIG
CONSTABLE
PIG PINK

"We can only understand the role of African Americans in the perpetuation of racist stereotypes in film and television in light of our country's history of race relations."

Jennifer Bloomquist, The Minstrel Legacy, 2015

## BLACK SNAFU

Anti-Blackness seems inescapably mixed into whatever context I place it into; literature, science, government, health, art... look into any "field" and see for yourself. My people have had to cry, scream, and fight for respect for centuries, and we still have not gained what we deserve. To move past the damage this has done to our society, we can't simply deny our history—we must recognize it. We must acknowledge the many ways in which this country has perpetuated a racial hierarchy since these lands were first colonized and stripped from indigenous peoples, and Black people were stolen from their native land and brought to America.

In BLACK SNAFU (Situation Niggas: All Fucked Up), I appropriate various depictions of Black people that I find throughout the history of cartooning and juxtapose them with photographs that celebrate and line up more authentically with my Black experience. The photographs I create vary in subject matter; I seek to include celebratory portraits, didactic still lives, and representational documentations of places rich in their relation to Black community, allowing me to fight back against the history of the racist caricature that I reclaim in my work. By combining these ambivalent visual languages, I intend to expose to viewers America's deplorable connection to anti-Black tropes through pop culture while simultaneously celebrating the reality of what it means to be Black.

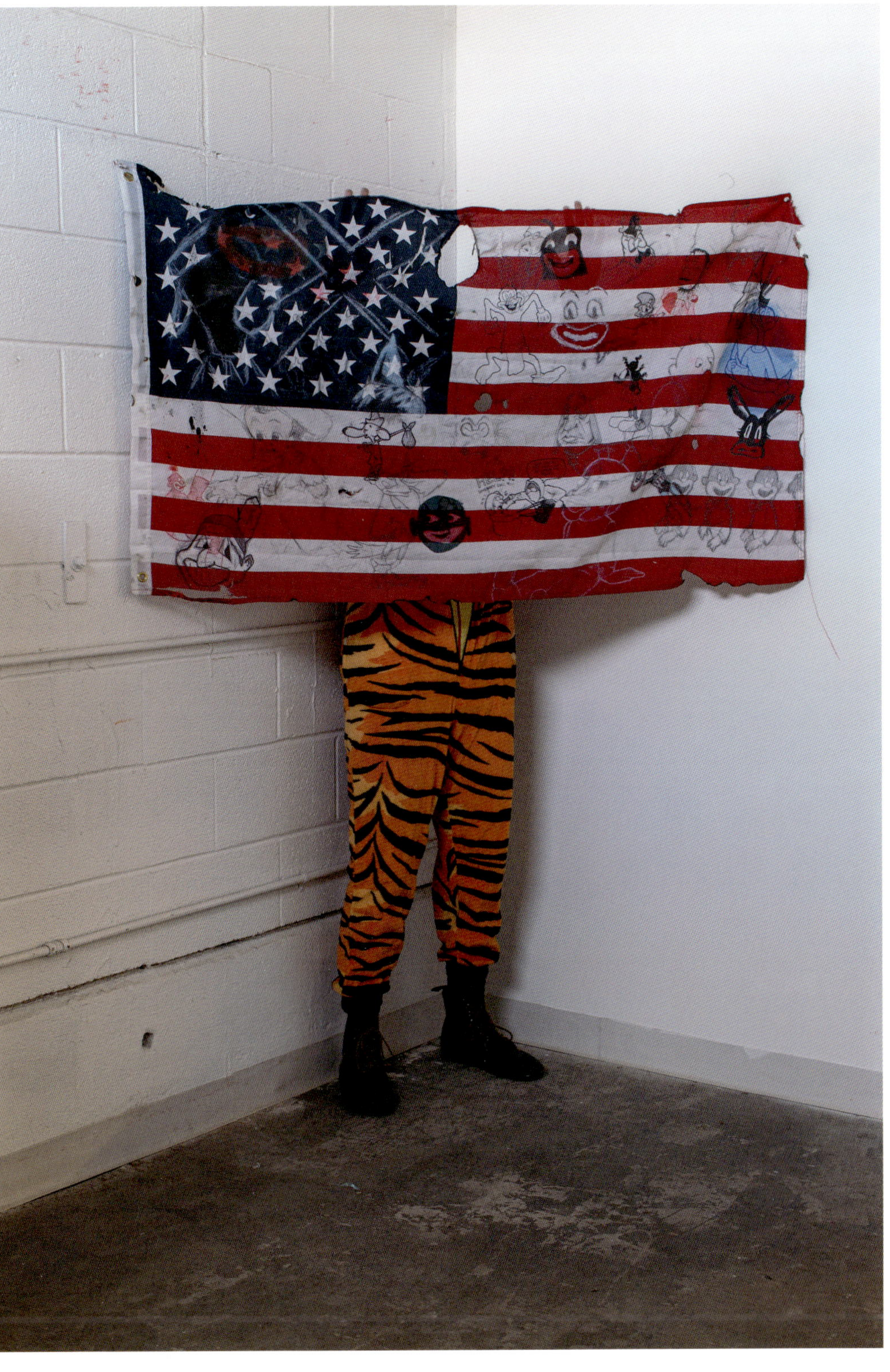

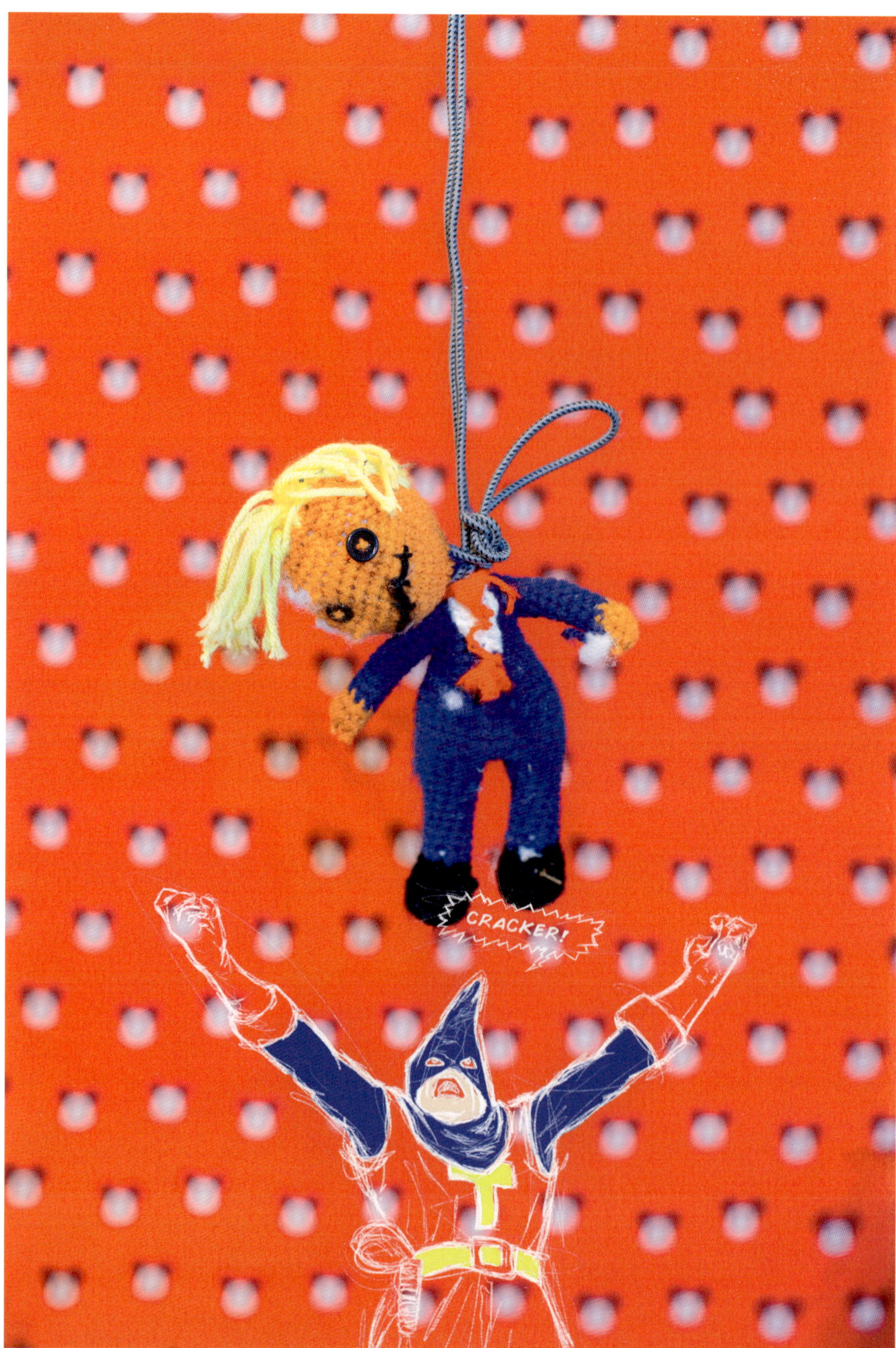
CRACKER!

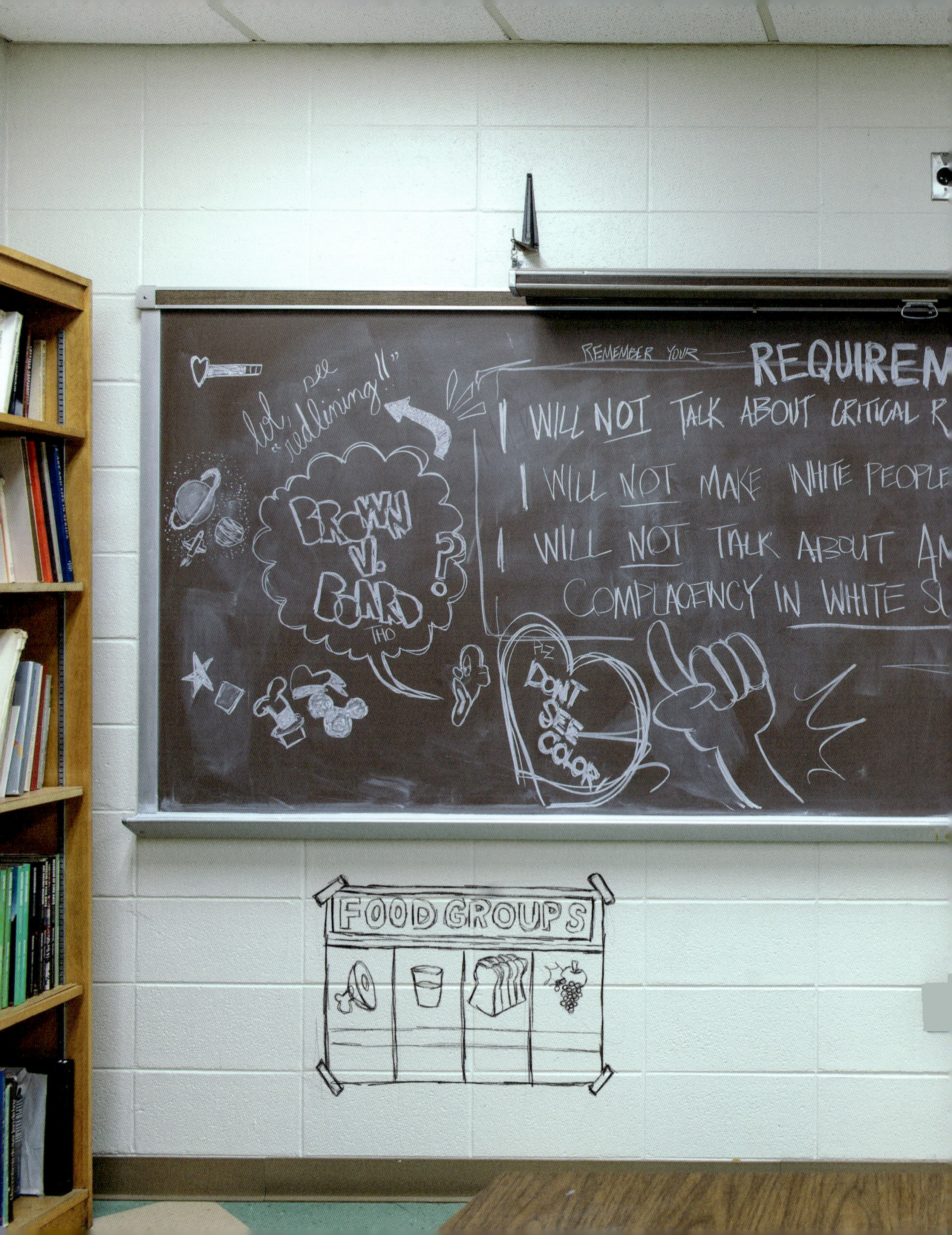

lol, see "redlining!!"
BROWN V. BOARD
THO
?!
REMEMBER YOUR REQUIREM
I WILL NOT TALK ABOUT CRITICAL R
I WILL NOT MAKE WHITE PEOPLE
I WILL NOT TALK ABOUT AM
COMPLACENCY IN WHITE S
PLZ
DONT SEE COLOR
FOOD GROUPS

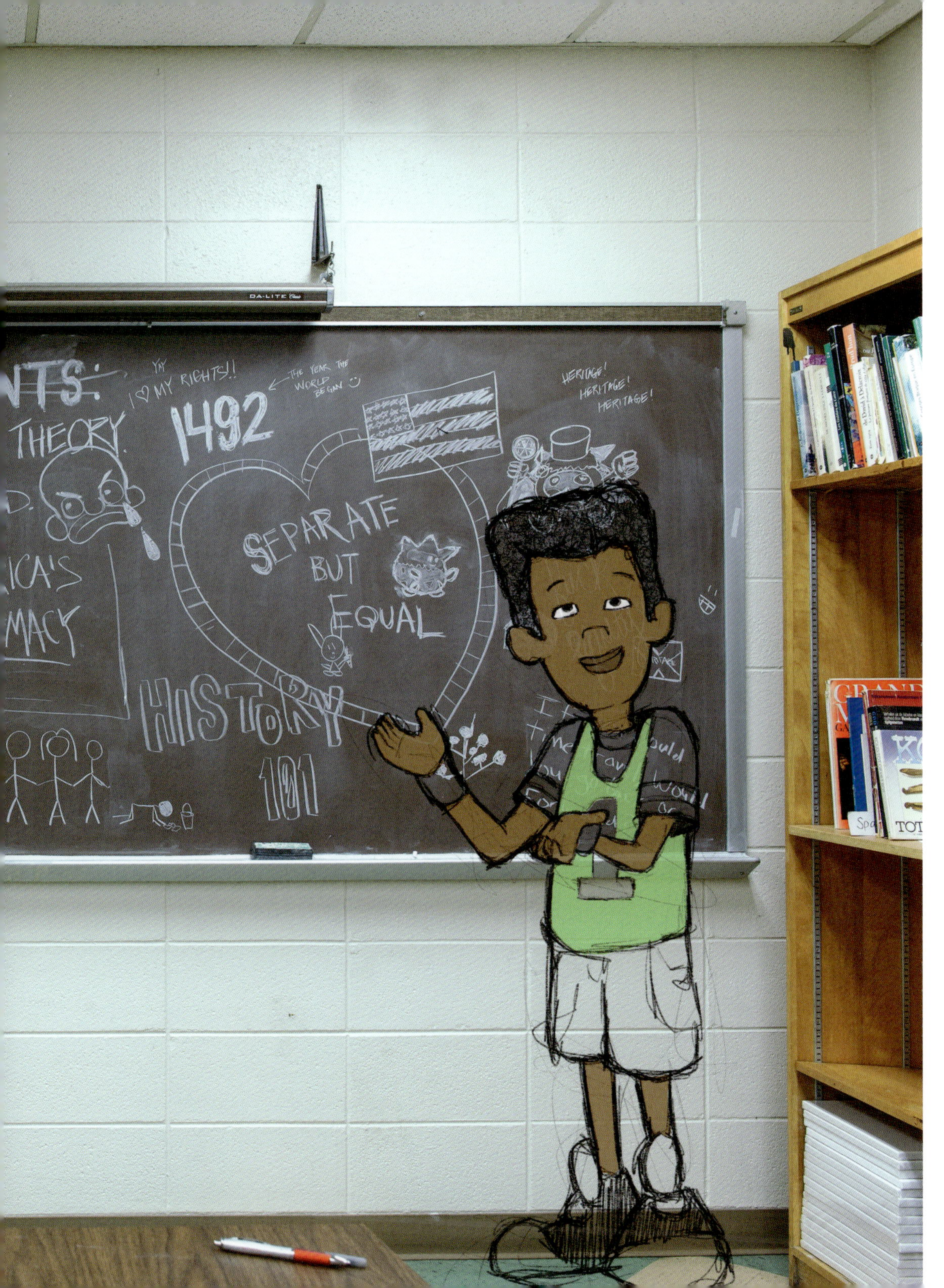

I ♡ MY RIGHTS!!
1492
THE YEAR THE WORLD BEGAN
THEORY
HERITAGE! HERITAGE! HERITAGE!
SEPARATE BUT EQUAL
HISTORY
101

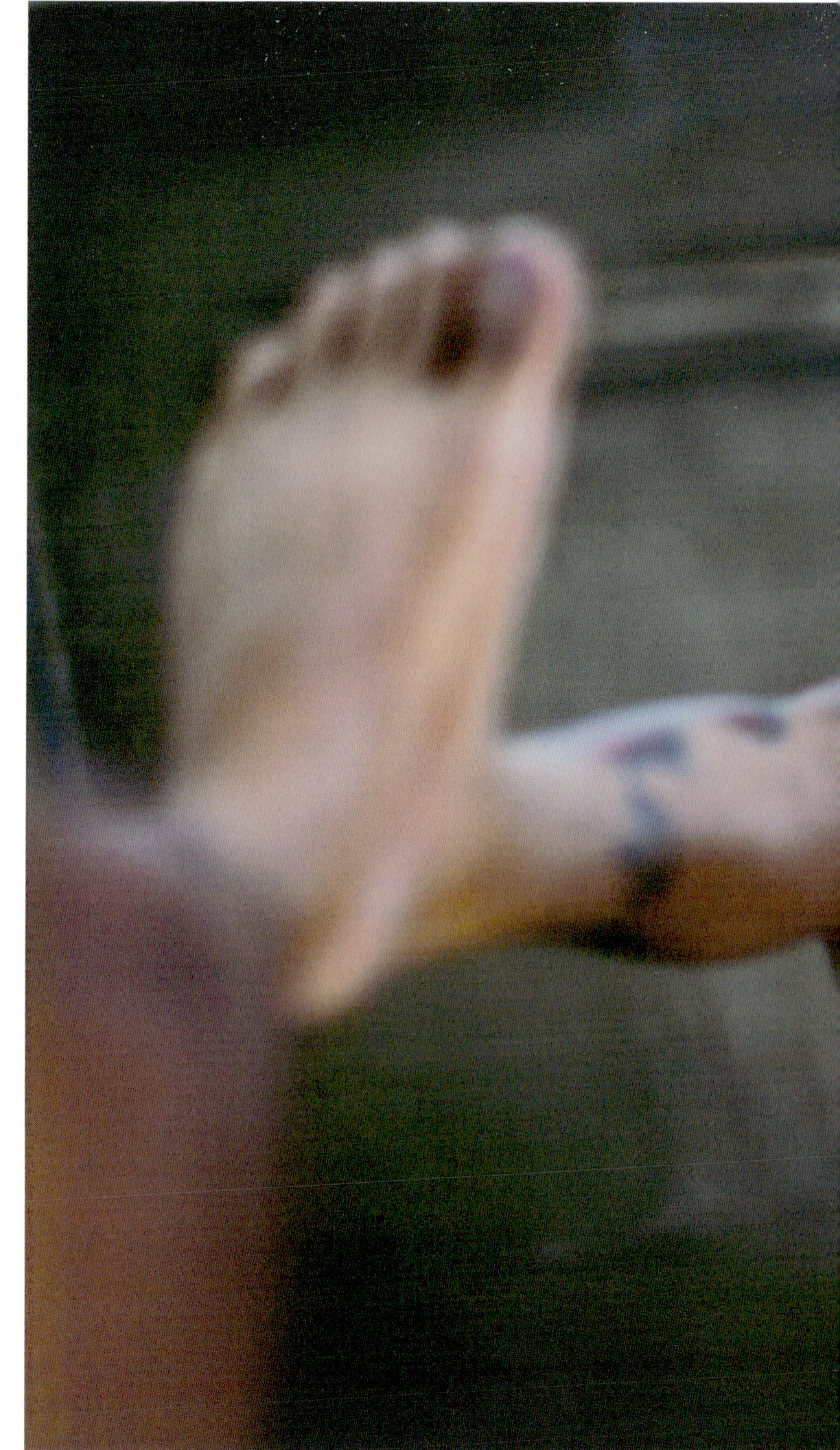

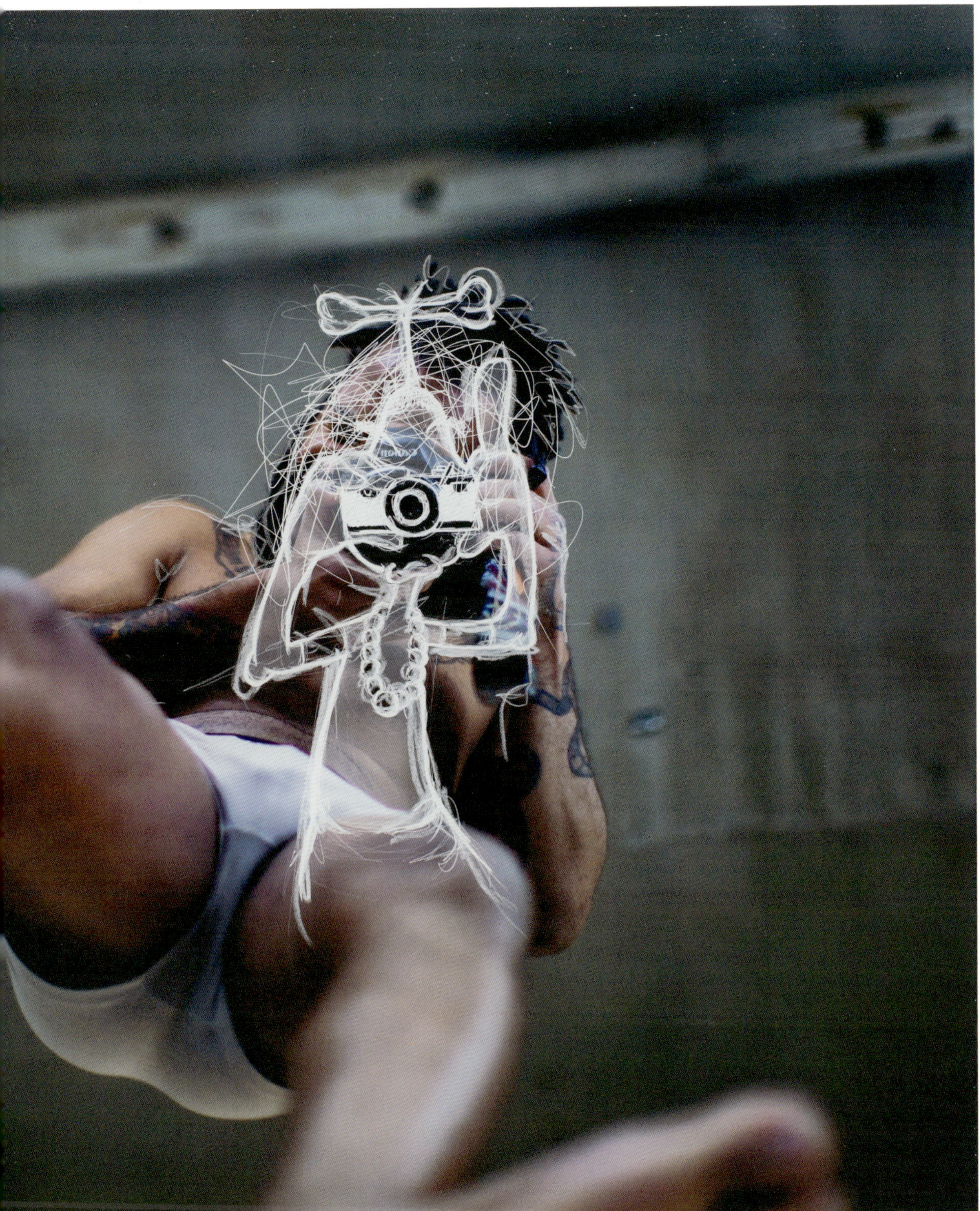

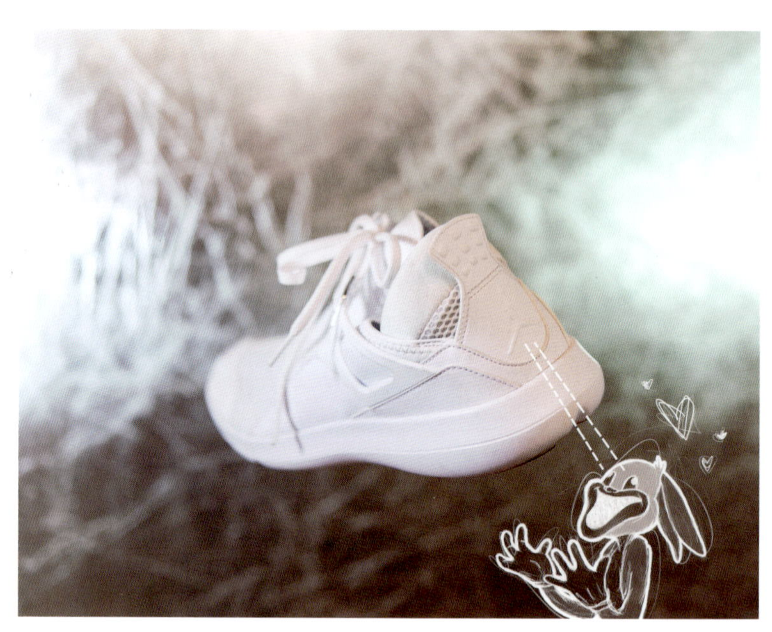

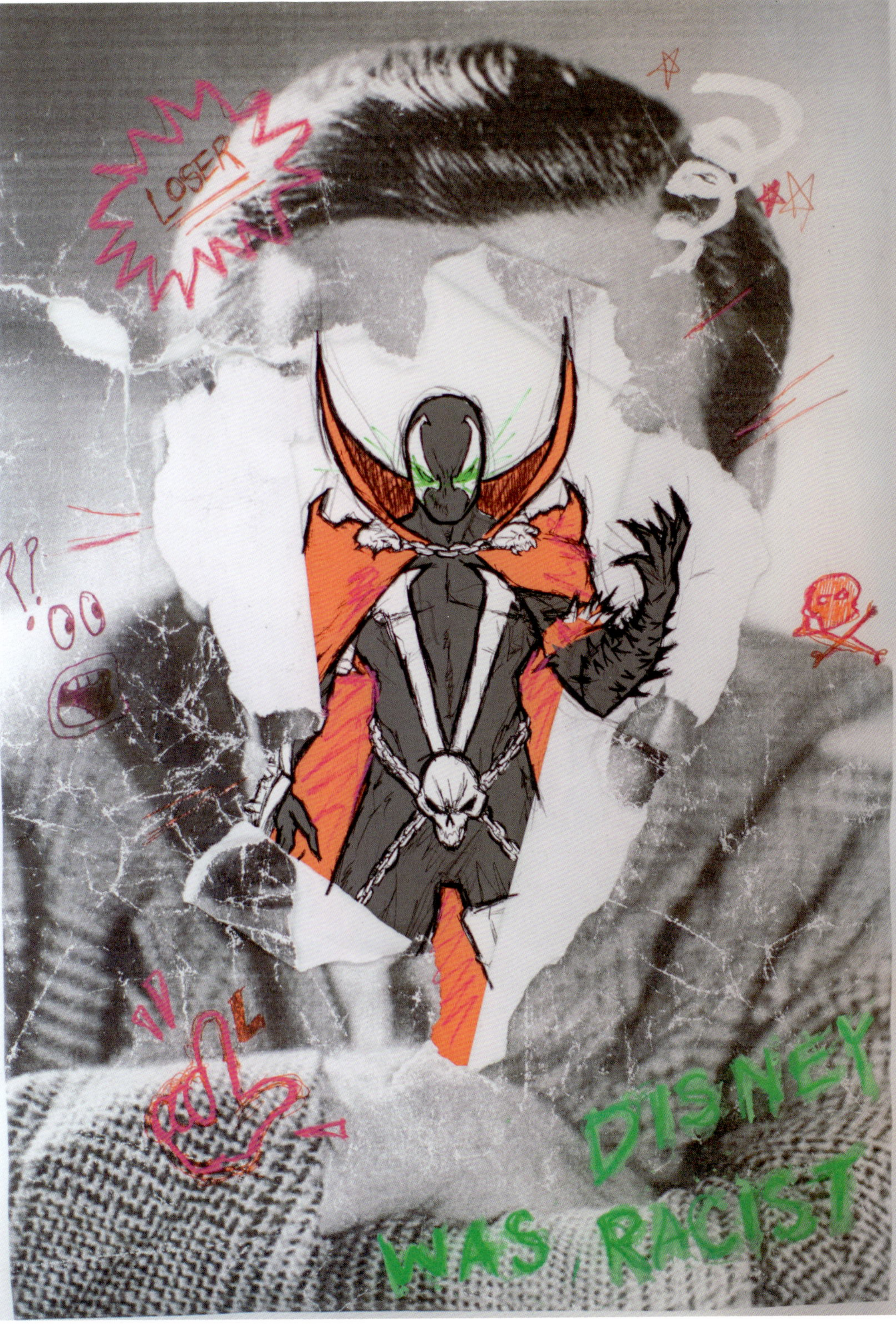
LOSER
DISNEY
WAS RACIST

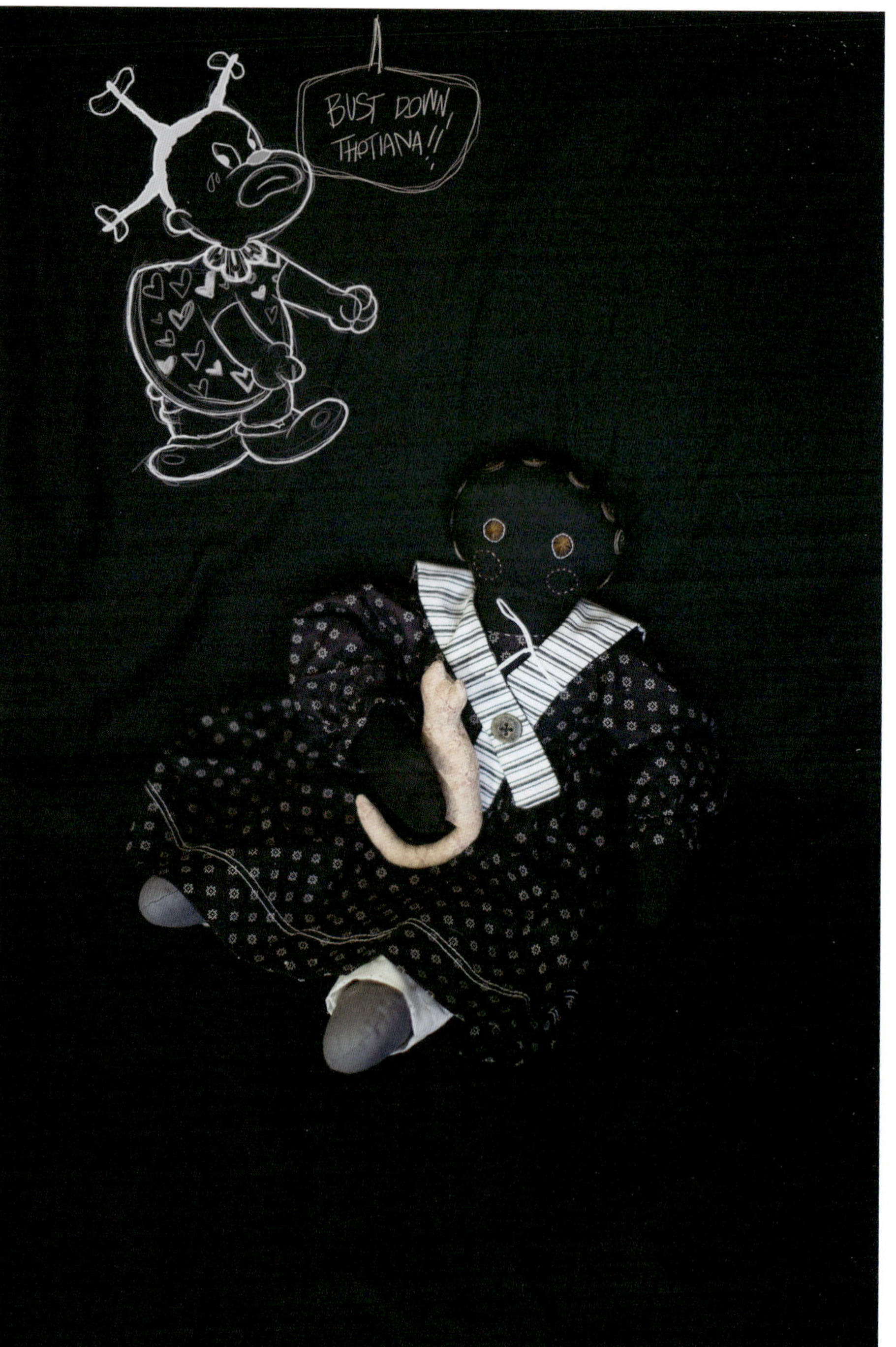
BUST DOWN, THOTIANA!!

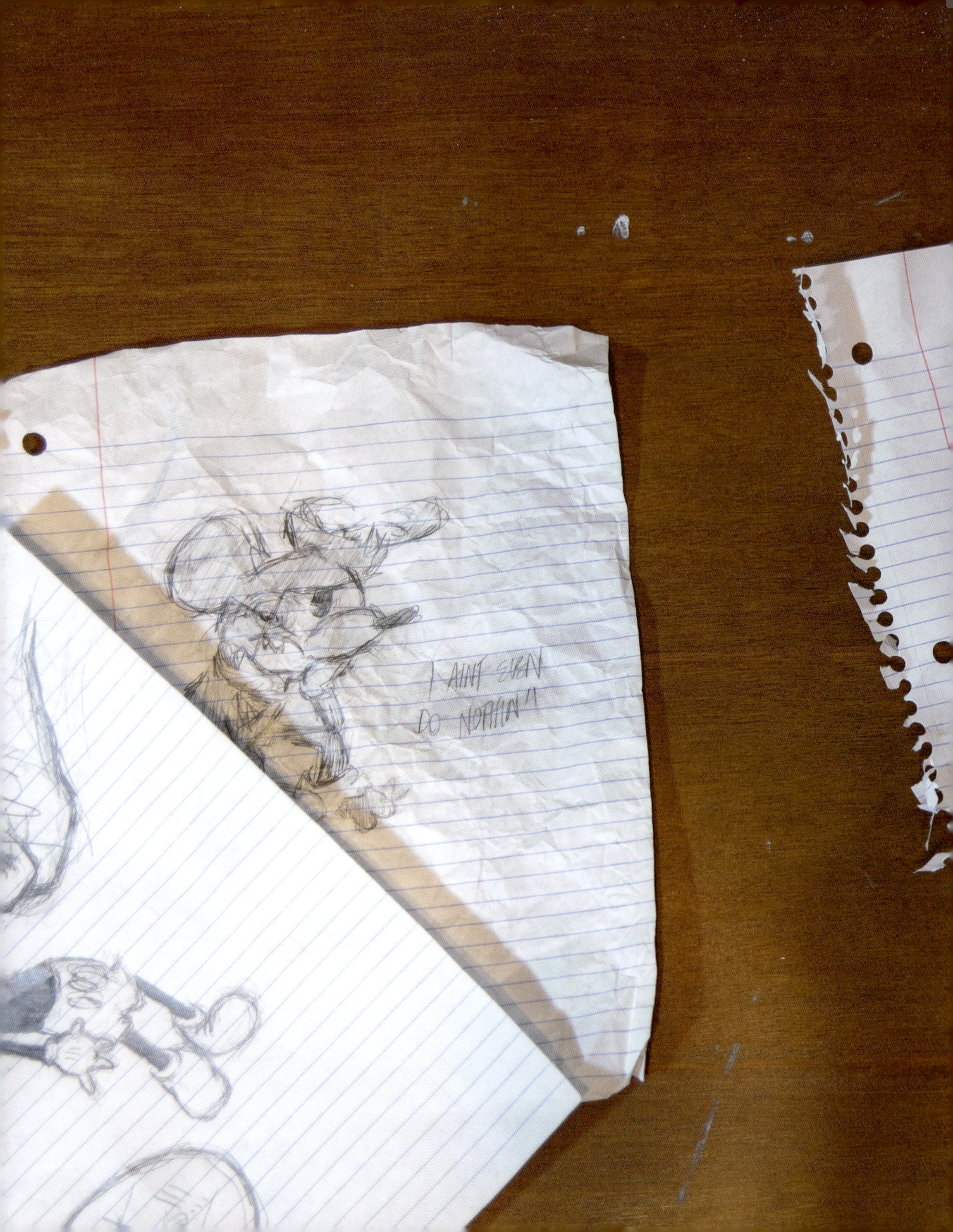
I AINT EVEN
DO NOTHIN'

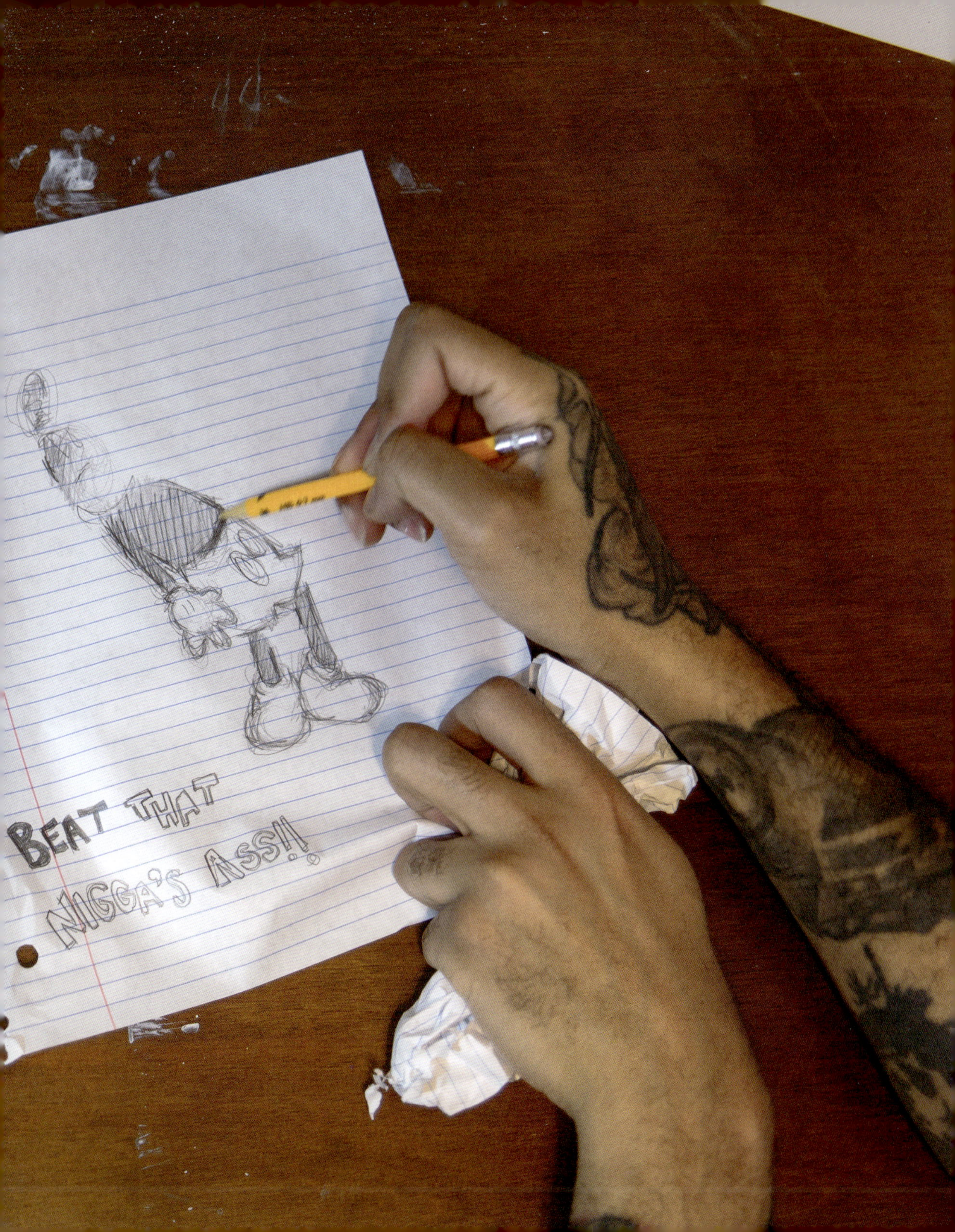
BEAT THAT
NIGGA'S ASS!!

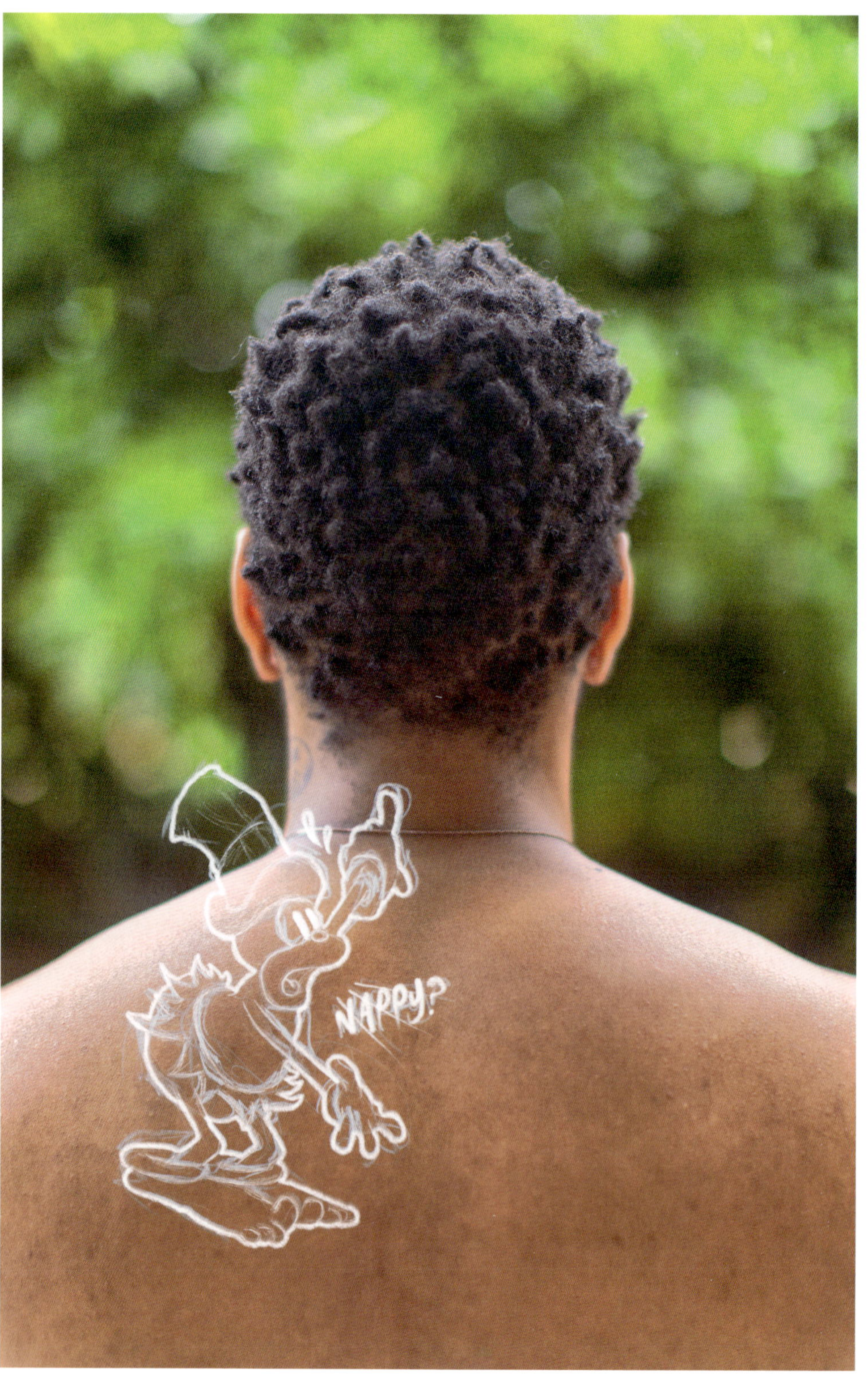
NAPPY?

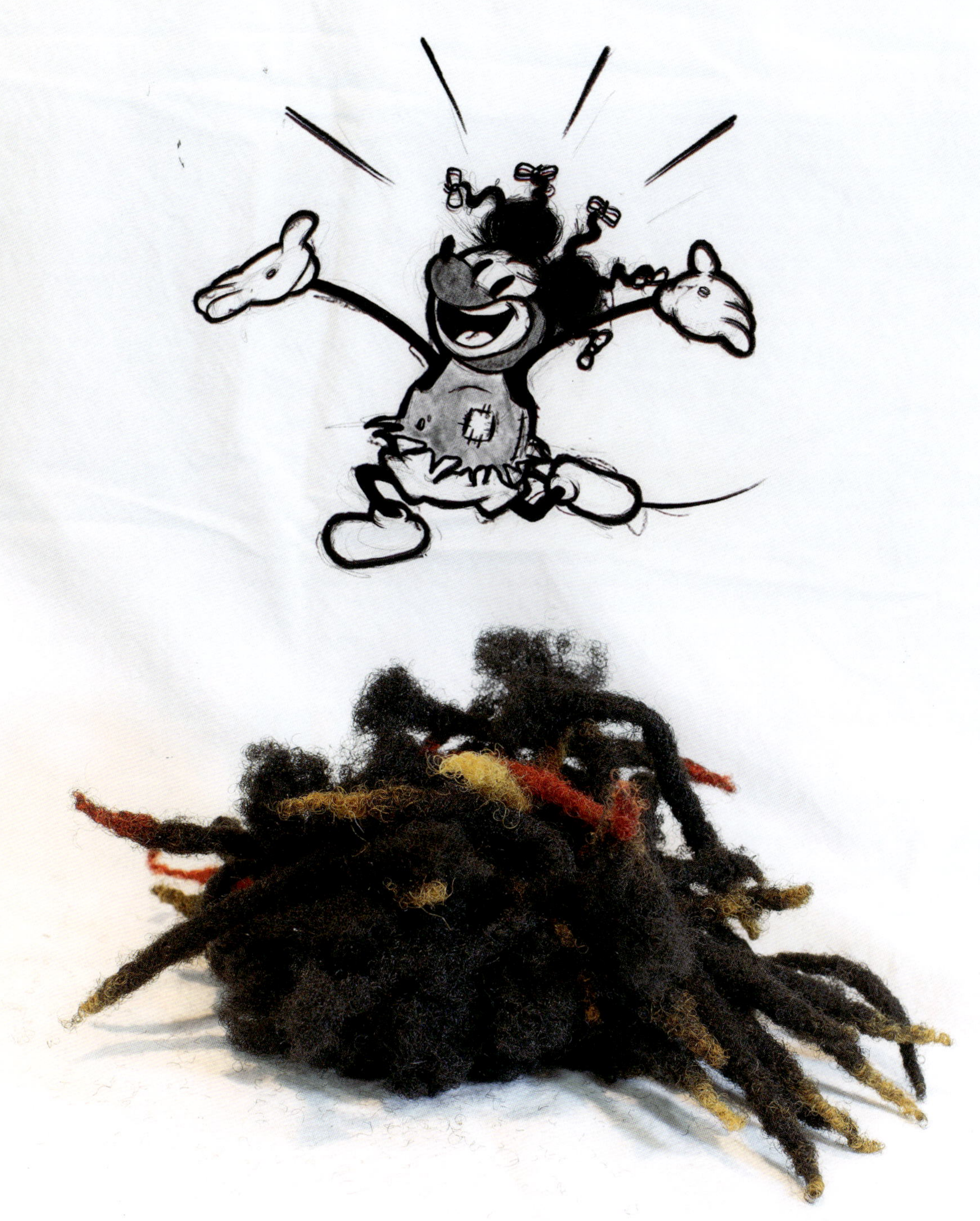

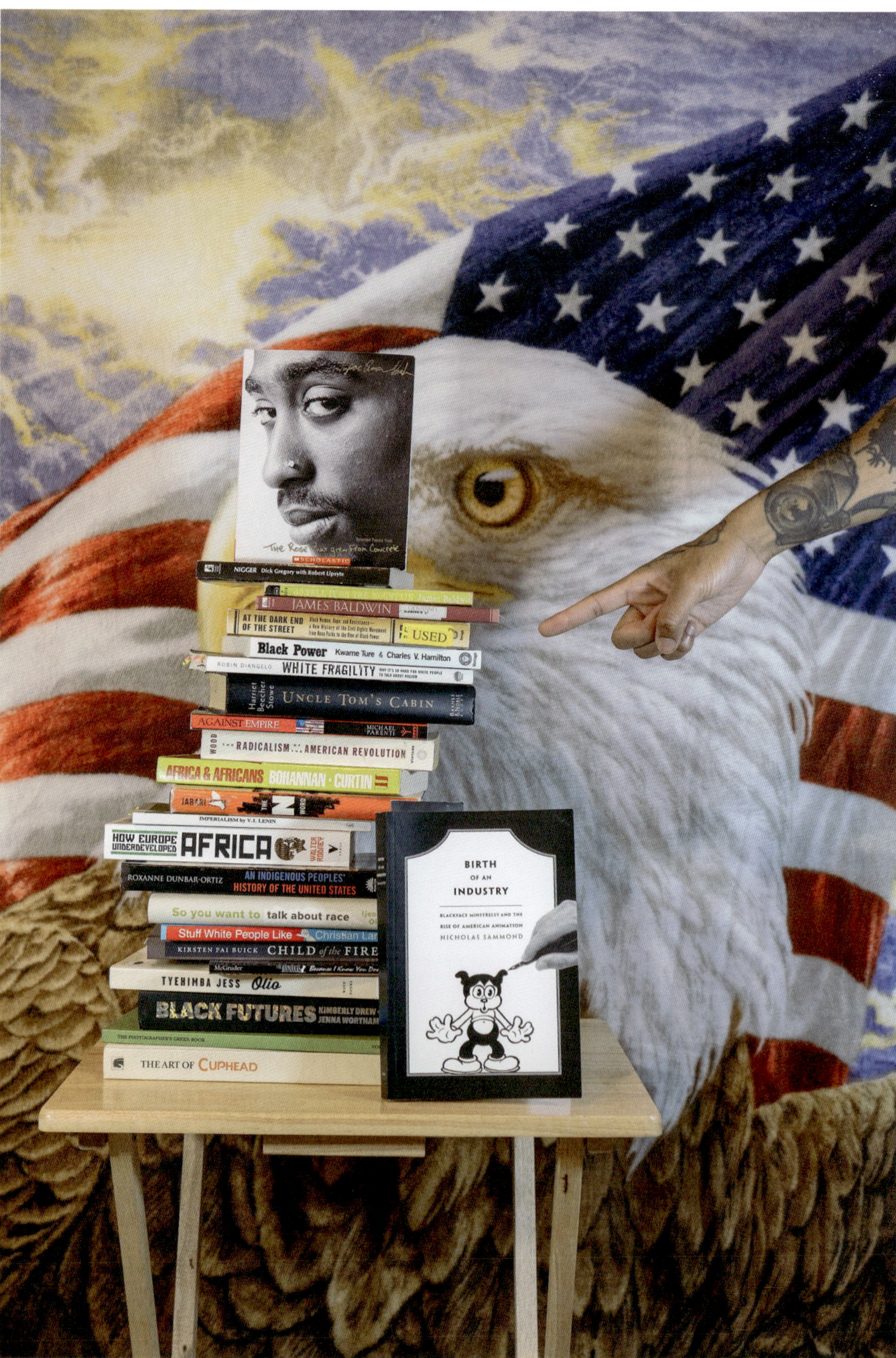
The Rose That Grew From Concrete
SCHOLASTIC
NIGGER Dick Gregory with Robert Lipsyte
JAMES BALDWIN
AT THE DARK END OF THE STREET
USED
Black Power Kwame Ture & Charles V. Hamilton
ROBIN DIANGELO WHITE FRAGILITY
Harriet Beecher Stowe UNCLE TOM'S CABIN
AGAINST EMPIRE MICHAEL PARENTI
WOOD
AMERICAN REVOLUTION
AFRICA & AFRICANS BOHANNAN · CURTIN
JABARI
THE N WORD
IMPERIALISM by V.I. LENIN
HOW EUROPE UNDERDEVELOPED AFRICA WALTER RODNEY
ROXANNE DUNBAR-ORTIZ AN INDIGENOUS PEOPLES' HISTORY OF THE UNITED STATES
So you want to talk about race
Stuff White People Like
KIRSTEN PAI BUICK CHILD of the FIRE
TYEHIMBA JESS Olio
BLACK FUTURES KIMBERLY DREW JENNA WORTHAM
THE PHOTOGRAPHER'S GREEN BOOK
THE ART OF CUPHEAD
BIRTH OF AN INDUSTRY
BLACKFACE MINSTRELSY AND THE RISE OF AMERICAN ANIMATION
NICHOLAS SAMMOND

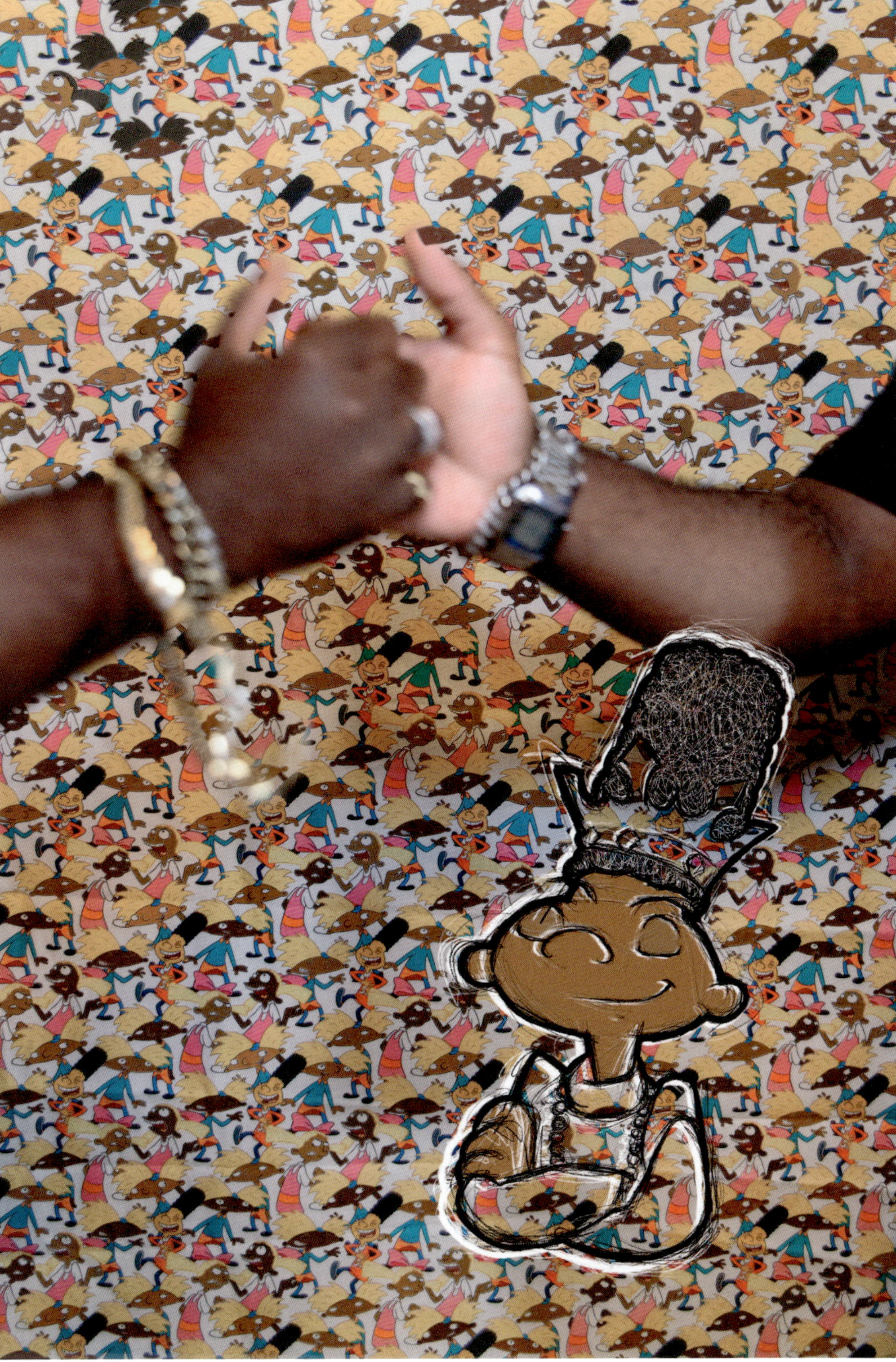

ood evening, I find myself, not for the first time, in the position of a kind of Jeremiah. For example, I don't disagree hat the inequality suffered by the American Negro population of the United States has hindered the American dream. Indeed, it has quarrell with some other things he has to say. The other, deeper, element of a certain awkwardness I feel has to do with one's poin of view. I have to put it that way – one's sense, one's system of reality. It would seem to me the proposition before the House, and would put it that way, is "the American Dream at the expense of the American Negro", or "the American Dream *is* at the expense o he American Negro". Is the question hideously loaded, and then one's response to that question – one's reaction to that questior – has to depend on effect and, in effect, where you find yourself in the world, what your sense of reality is, what your *system* o eality is. That is, it depends on assumptions which we hold so deeply so as to be scarcely aware of them. ... All white South Africar or Mississippi sharecropper, or Mississippi sheriff, or a Frenchman driven out of Algeria, all have, at bottom, a system of reality whicł compels them to, for example, in the case of the French exile from Algeria, to offend French reasons from having ruled Algeria. The Mississippi or Alabama sheriff, who really does believe, when he's facing a Negro boy or girl, that this woman, this man, this *child* must be insane to attack the system to which he owes his entire identity. Of course, to such a person, the proposition which we are rying to discuss here tonight does not exist. And on the other hand, I, have to speak as one of the people who've been most attackec by what we now must here call the Western or European system of reality. What white people in the world, what we call white supremacy – and I hate to say it here – comes from Europe. It's how it got to America. Beneath then, whatever one's reaction to this proposition is, has to be the question of whether or not civilizations can be considered, as such, equal, or whether one's civilizatior has the right to overtake and subjugate, and, in fact, to destroy another. Now, what happens when that happens? Leaving aside al he physical facts that one can quote. Leaving aside, rape or murder. Leaving aside the bloody catalog of oppression—which we are n one way too familiar with already—what this does to the subjugated, the most private, the most serious thing this does to the subjugated, is to destroy his sense of reality. It destroys, for example, his father's authority over him. His father can no longer tel him anything, because the past has disappeared, and his father has no power in the world. This means, in the case of an Americar Negro, born in that glittering republic, and the moment you are born, since you don't know any better, every stick and stone and ever face is white. And since you have not yet seen a mirror, you suppose that you are, too. It comes as a great shock around the age o 5, or 6, or 7, to discover that the flag to which you have pledged allegiance, along with everybody else, has not pledged allegiance to you. It comes as a great shock to discover that Gary Cooper killing off the Indians, when you were rooting for Gary Cooper, tha he Indians were you. It comes as a great shock to discover that the country which is your birthplace and to which you owe your life and your identity, has not, in its whole system of reality, evovled any place for you. The disaffection, the demoralization, and the gap between one person and another only on the basis of the color of their skin, begins there and accelerates – accelerates throughou a whole lifetime – to the present when you realize you're thirty and are having a terrible time managing to trust your countrymen. B he time you are thirty, you have been through a certain kind of mill. And the most serious effect of the mill you've been through is again, not the catalog of disaster, the policemen, the taxi drivers, the waiters, the landlady, the landlord, the banks, the insurance companies, the millions of details, twenty four hours of every day, which spell out to you that you are a worthless human being. It is not that. It's by that time that you've begun to see it happening, in your daughter or your son, or your niece or your nephew. You are hirty by now and nothing you have done has helped to escape the trap. But what is worse than that, is that nothing you have done and as far as you can tell, nothing you can do, will save your son or your daughter from meeting the same disaster and not impossibly coming to the same end. Now, we're speaking about expense. I suppose there are several ways to address oneself, to some attemp to find what that word means here. Let me put it this way, that from a very literal point of view, the harbors and the ports, and the railroads of the country–the economy, especially of the Southern states–could not conceivably be what it has become, if they hac not had, and do not still have, indeed for so long, for many generations, cheap labor. I am stating very seriously, and this is not ar overstatement: I picked the cotton, I carried it to the market, and I built the railroads under someone else's whip for nothing!! Fo nothing! ... The Southern oligarchy, which has still today so very much power in Washington, and therefore some power in the world was created by my labor and my sweat, and the violation of my women and the murder of my children. This, in the land of the free and the home of the brave.And no one can challenge that statement. It is a matter of historical record. In another way, this dream and we'll get to the dream in a moment, is at the expense of the American Negro. You watched this in the Deep South in great relief But not only in the Deep South. In the Deep South, you are dealing with a sheriff or a landlord, or a landlady or a girl of the Westerr Union desk, and she doesn't know quite who she's dealing with, by which I mean, that if you're not a part of the town, and if you are a Nothern Nigger, it shows in millions of ways. So she simply knows that it's an unknown quantity, and she wants to have nothing to do with it because she won't talk to you, you have to wait for a while to get your telegram. OK, we all know this. We've all been througl it and, by the time you get to be a man, it's very easy to deal with. But what is happening in the poor woman, the poor man's minc is this: they've been raised to believe, and by now they helplessly believe, that no matter how terrible their lives may be, and thei lives have been quite terrible, and no matter how far they fall, no matter what disaster overtakes them, they have one enormous knowledge in consolation, which is like a heavenly revelation: at least, they are not Black. Now, I suggest that of all the terrible things that can happen to a human being, that is one of the worst. I suggest that what has happened to white Southerners is in some ways after all, much worse than what has happened to Negroes there because Sheriff Clark in Selma, Alabama, cannot be considered – you know, no one can be dismissed as a total monster. I'm sure he loves his wife, his children. I'm sure, you know, he likes to ge drunk. You know, after all, one's got to assume he is visibly a man like me. But he doesn't know what drives him to use the club, to menace with the gun and to use the cattle prod. Something awful must have happened to a human being to be able to put a cattle prod against a woman's breasts, for example! What happens to the woman is ghastly. What happens to the man who does it is in some ways much, much worse. This is being done, after all, not a hundred years ago, but [illegible] in a country which is blessed with what we call prosperity, a word we won't examine too closely; with a certain kind of social coherence, which calls itself a civilizec nation, and which espouses the notion of the freedom of the world. And it is perfectly true from the point of view now simply of ar American Negro. Any American Negro watching this, no matter where he is, from the vantage point of Harlem, which is anothe terrible place, has to say to himself, in spite of what the government says – the government says we can't do anything about it – bu if those were white people being murdered in Mississippi work farms, being carried off to jail, if those were white children running up and down the streets, the government would find some way of doing something about it. We have a civil rights bill now where ar amendment, the fifteenth amendment, [illegible] I hate to sound again like an Old Testament prophet – but i he amendment was not honored then, I would have any reason to believe in the civil rights bill will be honored now. And after al ameone's been there, since before, you know, a lot of other people got there. If one has got to prove one's title to the land, isn't four hundred years enough? Four hundred years? At least three wars? The American soil is full of the corpses of my ancestors. Why is my freedom or my citizenship, or my right to live there, how is it conceivably a question now? And I suggest further, and in the same way, the moral life of Alabama sheriffs and poor Alabama ladies – white ladies – their moral lives have been destroyed by the plague called color, that the American sense of reality has been corrupted by it. At the risk of sounding excessive, what I always felt, when I finally left the country, and found myself abroad, in other places, and watched the Americans abroad – and these are my countrymen – and I do care about them, and even if I didn't, there is something between us. We have the same shorthand, I know, if I look at a boy or a girl from Tennessee, where they came from in Tennessee and what that means. No Englishman knows that. No Frenchman, no one in the world knows that, except another Black man who comes from the same place. One watches these lonely people denying the only kin they have. We talk about integration in America as though it was some great new conundrum. The problem in America is that we've been integrated for a very long time. Put me next to any African and you will see what I mean. My grandmother was not a rapist. What we are not facing is the result of what we've done. What one brings the American people to do for all our sakes is simply to accept our history. I was there not only as a slave, but also as a concubine. One knows the power, after all, which can be used against another person if you've got absolute power over that person. It seemed to me when I watched Americans in Europe what they didn't know about Europeans was what they didn't know about me. They weren't trying, for example, to be nasty to the French girl, or rude to the French waiter. They didn't know they hurt their feelings. They didn't have any sense this particular woman, this particular man, though they spoke another language and had different manners and ways, was a human being. And they walked over them, the same kind of bland ignorance, condescension, charming and cheerful with which they've always pat me on the head and called me "Shine" and were upset when I was upset. What is relevant about this is that whereas [illegible] when I was born, the question of having to deal with what is unspoken by the subjugated, what is never said to the master, of ever having to deal with this reality was a very remote possibility. It was in no one's mind. When I was growing up, I was taught in American history books, that Africa had no history, and neither did I. That I was a savage about whom the less said, the better, who had been saved by Europe and brought to America. And, of course, I believed it. I didn't have much choice. Those were the only books there were. Everyone else seemed to agree. If you walk out of Harlem, ride out of Harlem, downtown, the world agrees what you see is much bigger, cleaner, whiter, richer, safer than where you are. They collect the garbage. People obviously can pay their life insurance. Their children look happy, safe. You're not. And you go back home, and it would seem that, of course, that it's an act of God that this is true! That you belong where white people have put you. It is only since the Second World War that there's been a counter-image in the world. And that image did not come about through any legislation or part of any American government, but through the fact that Africa was suddenly on the stage of the world, and Africans had to be dealt with in a way they'd never been dealt with before. This gave an American Negro for the first time a sense of himself beyond the savage or a clown. It has created and will create a great many conundrums. One of the great things that the white world does not know, but I think I do know, is that Black people are just like everybody else. One has used the myth of Negro and the myth of color to pretend and to assume that you were dealing with, essentially, with something exotic, bizarre, and practically, according to human laws, unknown. Alas, it is not true. We're also mercenaries, dictators, murderers, liars. We are human too. What is crucial here is that unless we can manage to accept, establish some kind of dialog between those people whom I *pretend* have paid for the American dream and those other people who have not achieved it, we will be in terrible trouble. I want to say, at the end, the last, is that is that is what concerns me most. We are sitting in this room, and we are all, at least I'd like to think we are, relatively civilized, and we can talk to each other at least on certain levels so that we could walk out of here assuming that the measure of our enlightenment, or at least, our politeness, has some effect on the world. It may not. [illegible] for example, when the ex-Attorney General, Mr. Robert Kennedy, said that it was conceivable that in forty years, in America, we might have a Negro president. That sounded like a very emancipated statement, I suppose, to white people. They were not in Harlem when this statement was first heard. And they're not here, and possibly will never hear the laughter and the bitterness, and the scorn with which this statement was greeted. From the point of view of the man in the Harlem barber shop, Bobby Kennedy only got here yesterday, and he's already on his way to the presidency. We've been here for four hundred years and now he tells us that maybe in forty years, if you're good, we may let you become president. What is dangerous here is the turning away from – the turning away from – anything any white American says. The reason for the political hesitation, in spite of the Johnson landslide is that one has been betrayed by American politicians for so long. And I am [illegible] grown [illegible] and perhaps I can be reasoned with. I certainly hope I can be. But I don't know, and [illegible] none of us know how to deal with those other people whom the white world has so long ignored, who don't believe anything the white world says and don't entirely believe anything I [illegible] say [illegible]. And one can't blame them. You watch what has happened to them in less than twenty years. It seems to me that the City of New York, for example – this is my last point – it's had Negroes in it for a very long time. If the city of New York were able, as it has indeed been able, in the last fifteen years to reconstruct itself, tear down buildings and raise great new ones, downtown and for money, and has done nothing whatever except build housing projects in the ghetto for the Negroes. And of course, Negroes hate it. Presently the property does indeed deteriorate because the children cannot bear it. They want to get out of the ghetto. If the American pretensions were based on more solid, a more honest assessment of life and of themselves, it would not mean for Negroes when someone says "Urban Renewal" that Negroes simply are going to be thrown out into the streets. This is just what it does mean now. This is not an act of God. We're dealing with a society made and ruled by men. Had the American Negro not been present in America, I am convinced the history of the American labor movement would be much more edifying than it is. It is a terrible thing for an entire people to surrender to the notion that one-ninth of its population is beneath them. And until that moment, until the moment comes when we, the Americans, we, the American people, are able to accept the fact, that I have to accept, for example, that my ancestors are both white and Black; that on that continent we are trying to forge a new identity for which we need each other and that I am not a ward of America, that I am not an object of missionary charity, that I am one of the people who built the country—until this moment there is scarcely any hope for the American dream, because the people who are denied participation in it, by their very presence, will wreck it. And if that happens it is a very grave moment for the West.

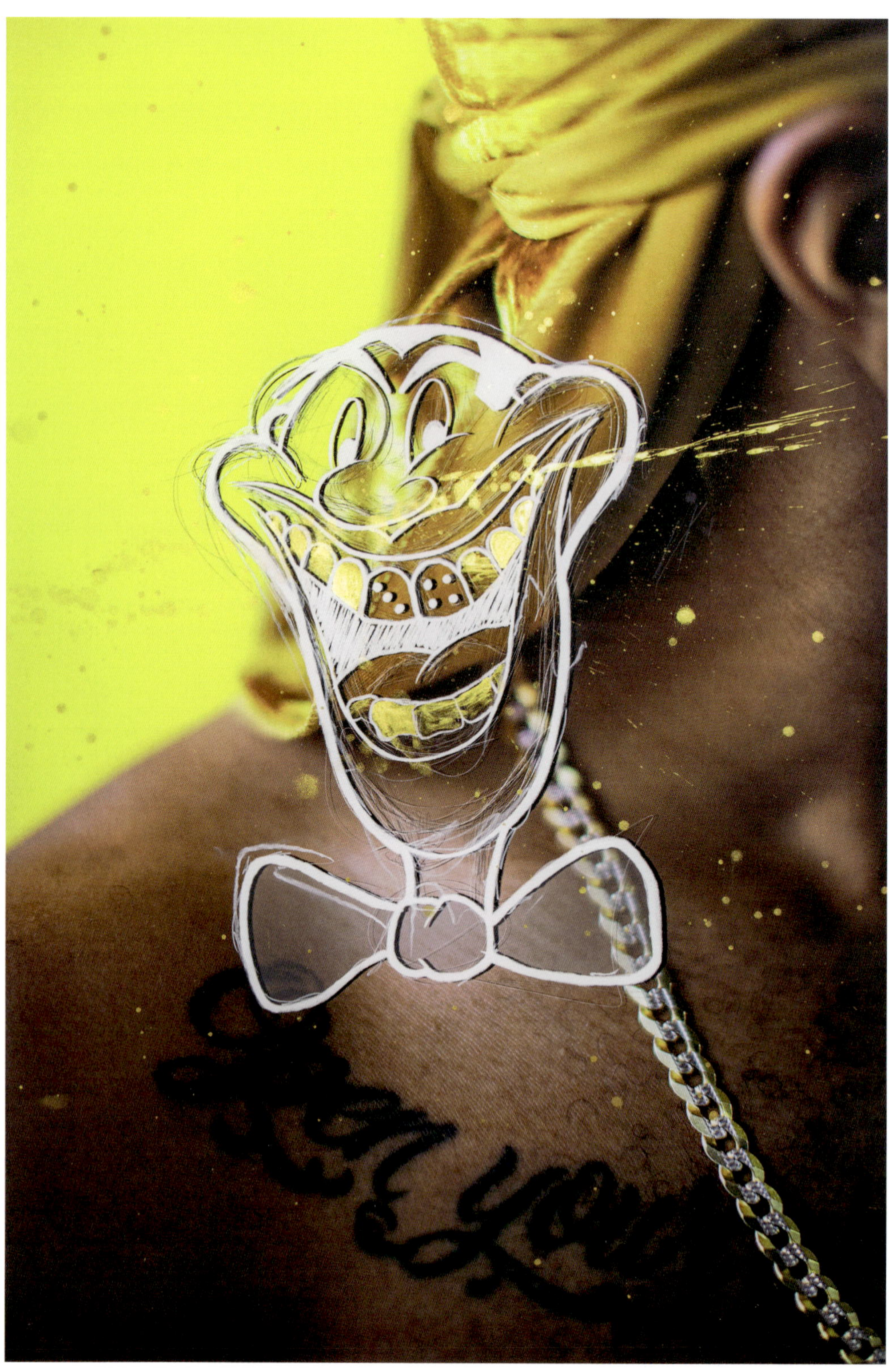

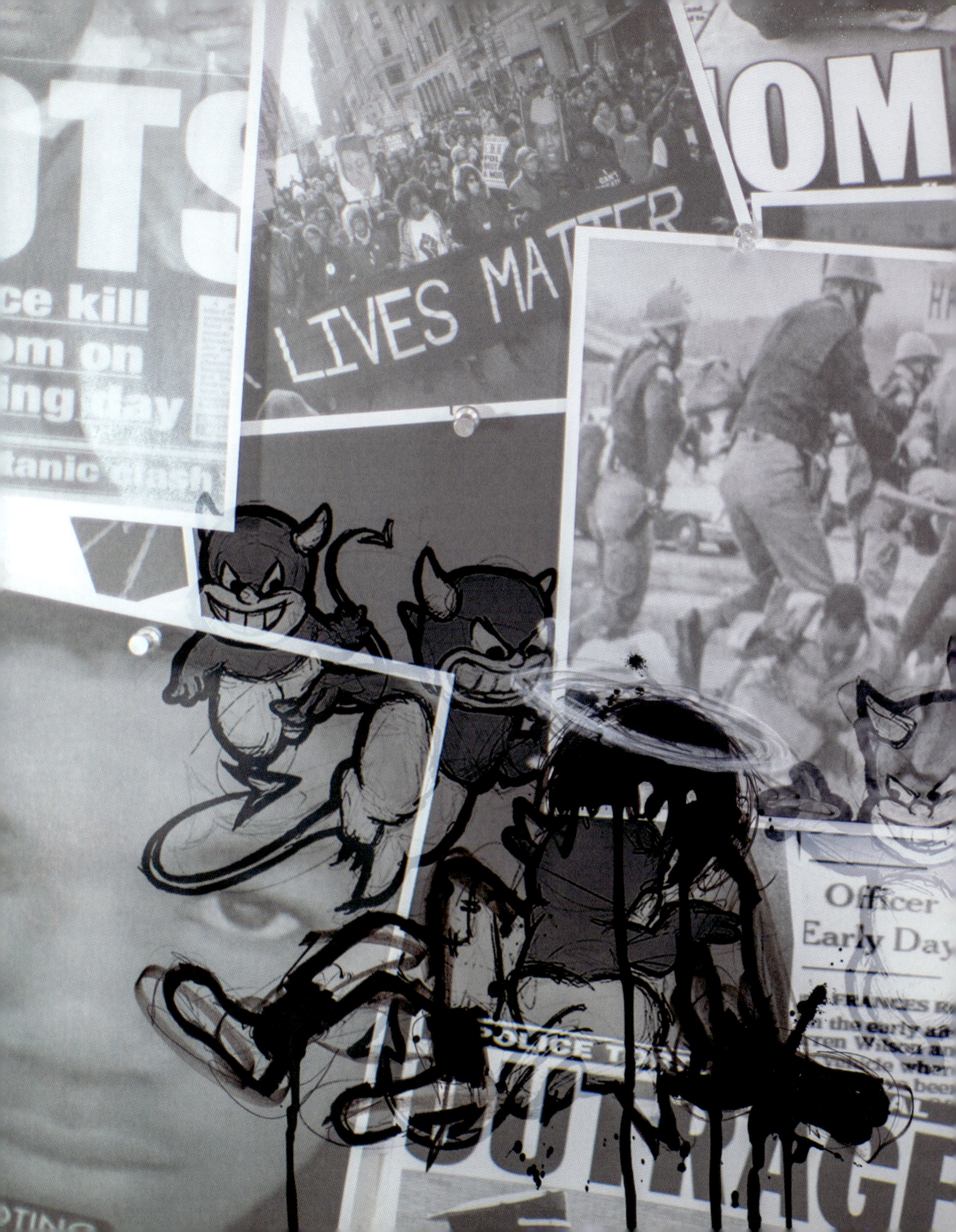

ce kill
om on
ing day
tanic clash
LIVES MATTER
Officer
Early Day
POLICE TO

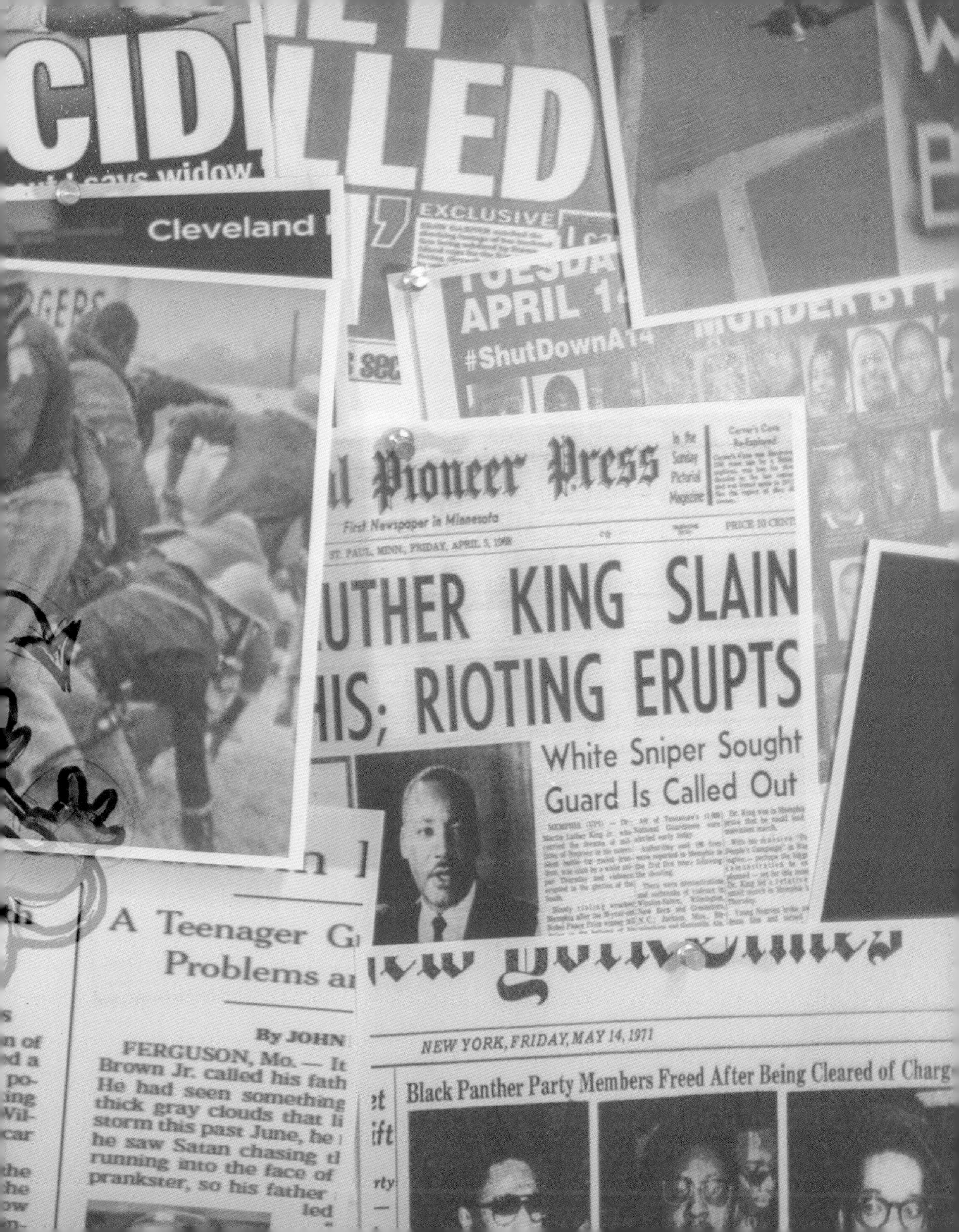

CIDI

Leaves widow

LLED

EXCLUSIVE

Cleveland

TUESDA

APRIL 14

#ShutDownA14

Carver's Cave Re-Explored

ul Pioneer Press

In the Sunday Pictorial Magazine

First Newspaper in Minnesota

PRICE 10 CENT

ST. PAUL, MINN., FRIDAY, APRIL 5, 1968

LUTHER KING SLAIN
HIS; RIOTING ERUPTS

White Sniper Sought
Guard Is Called Out

A Teenager G
Problems a

By JOHN

FERGUSON, Mo. — It
Brown Jr. called his fath
He had seen something
thick gray clouds that li
storm this past June, he
he saw Satan chasing th
running into the face of
prankster, so his father
led

NEW YORK, FRIDAY, MAY 14, 1971

Black Panther Party Members Freed After Being Cleared of Charg

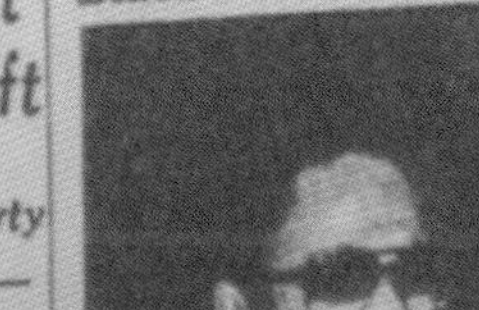

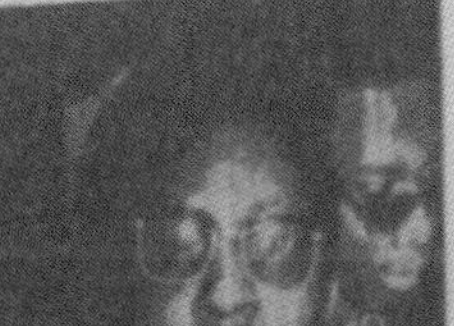

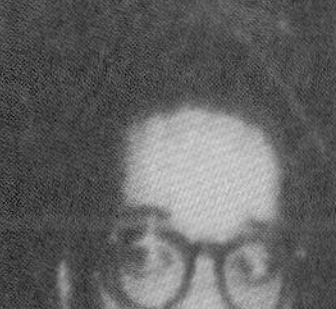

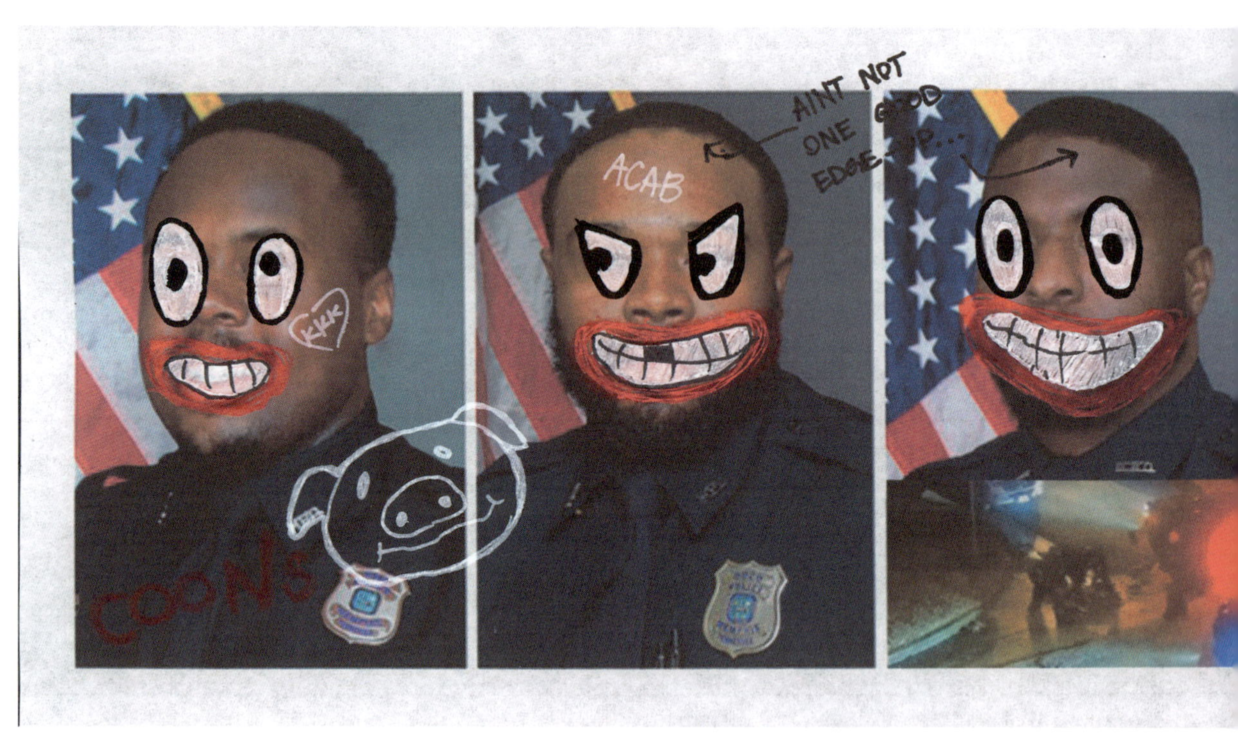
KKK
COONS
ACAB
AINT NOT ONE GOOD EDGE UP...

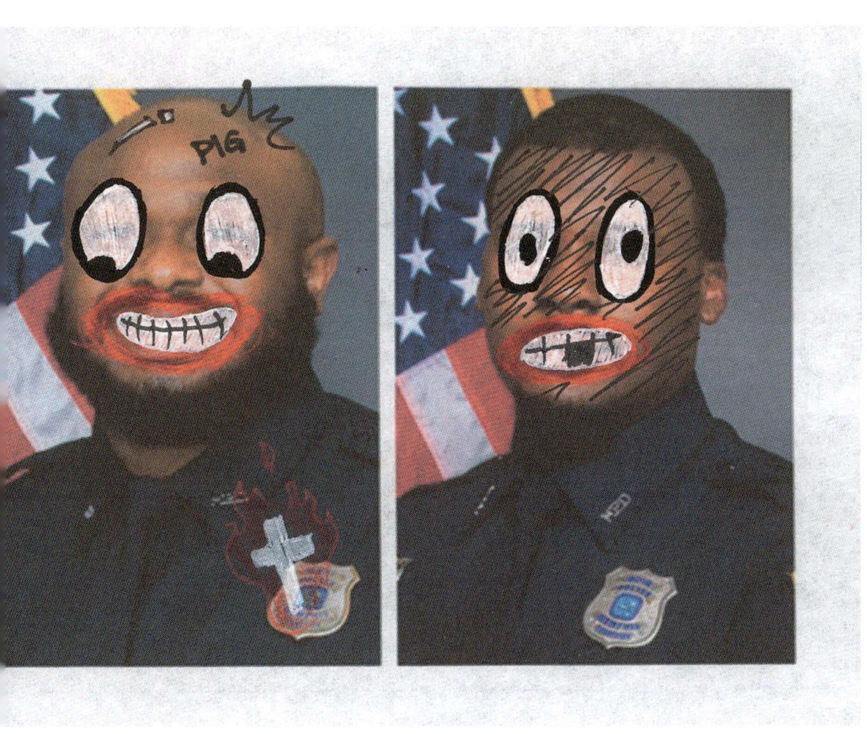
PIG

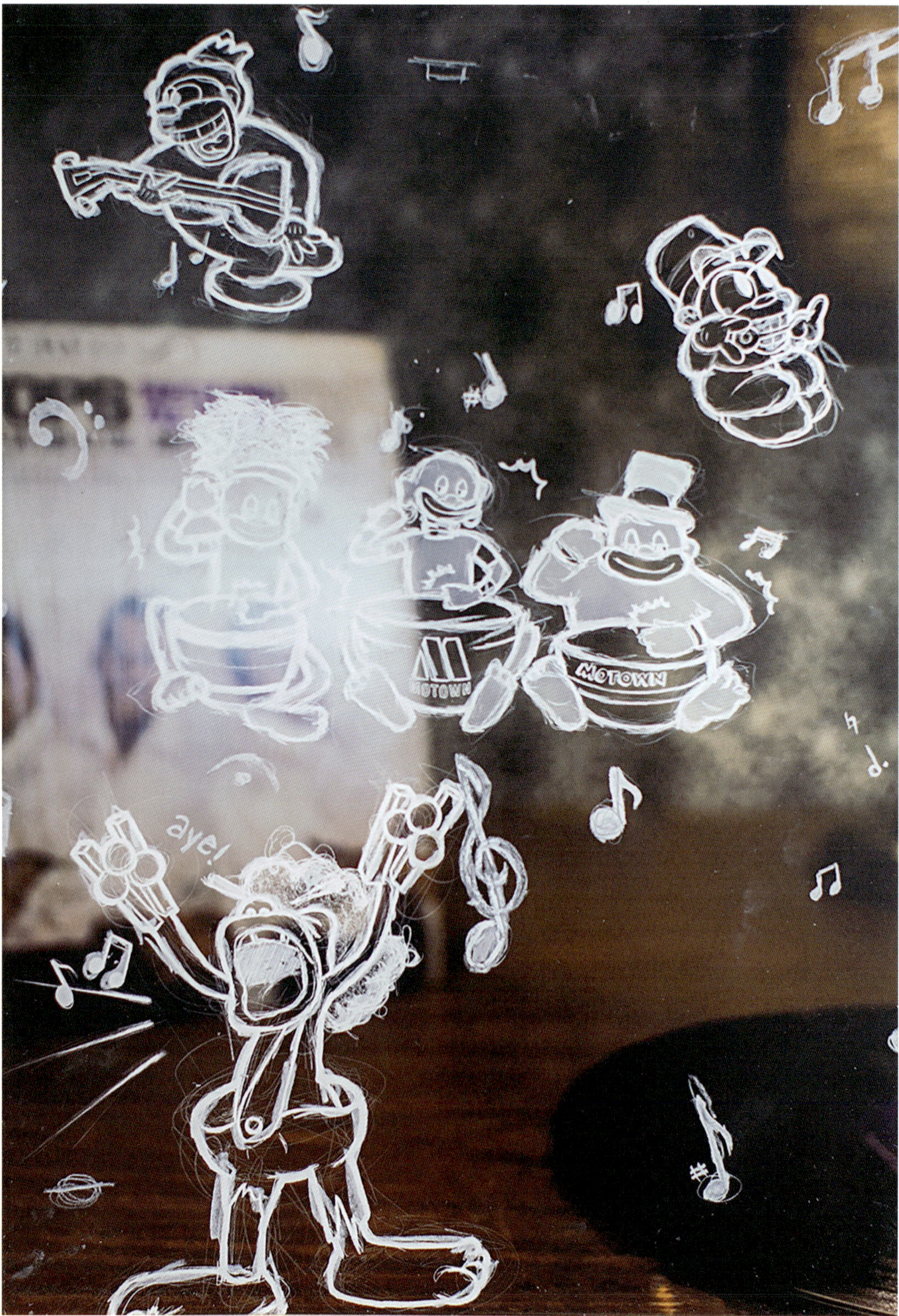
aye!
MOTOWN

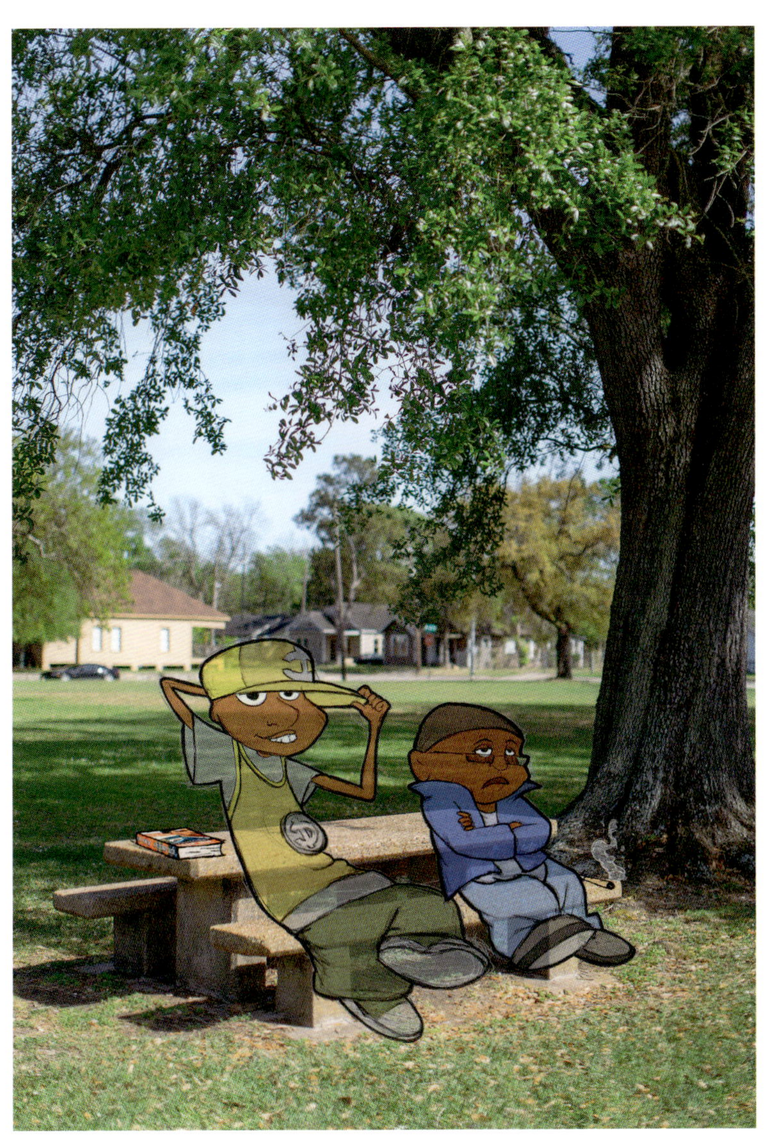

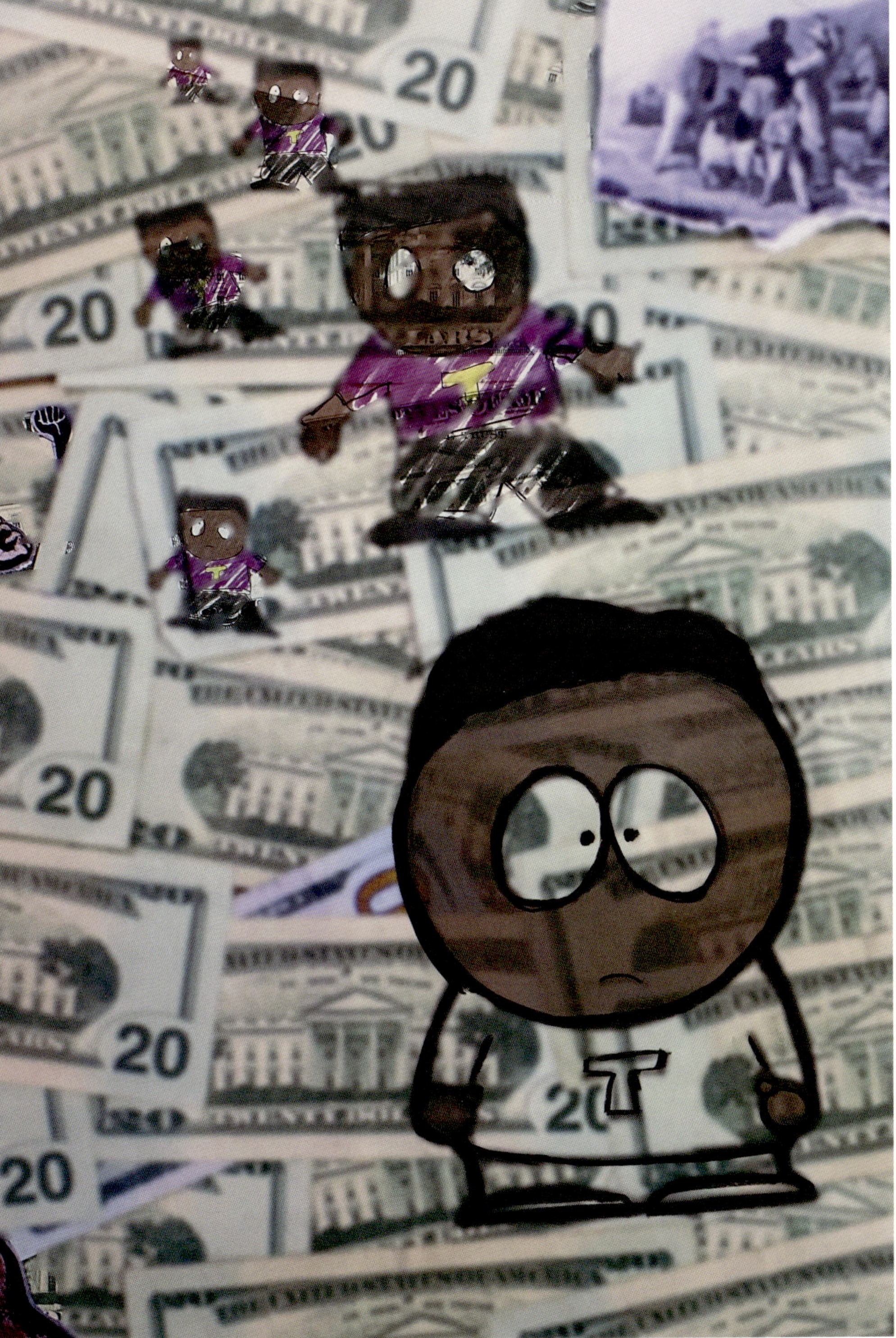

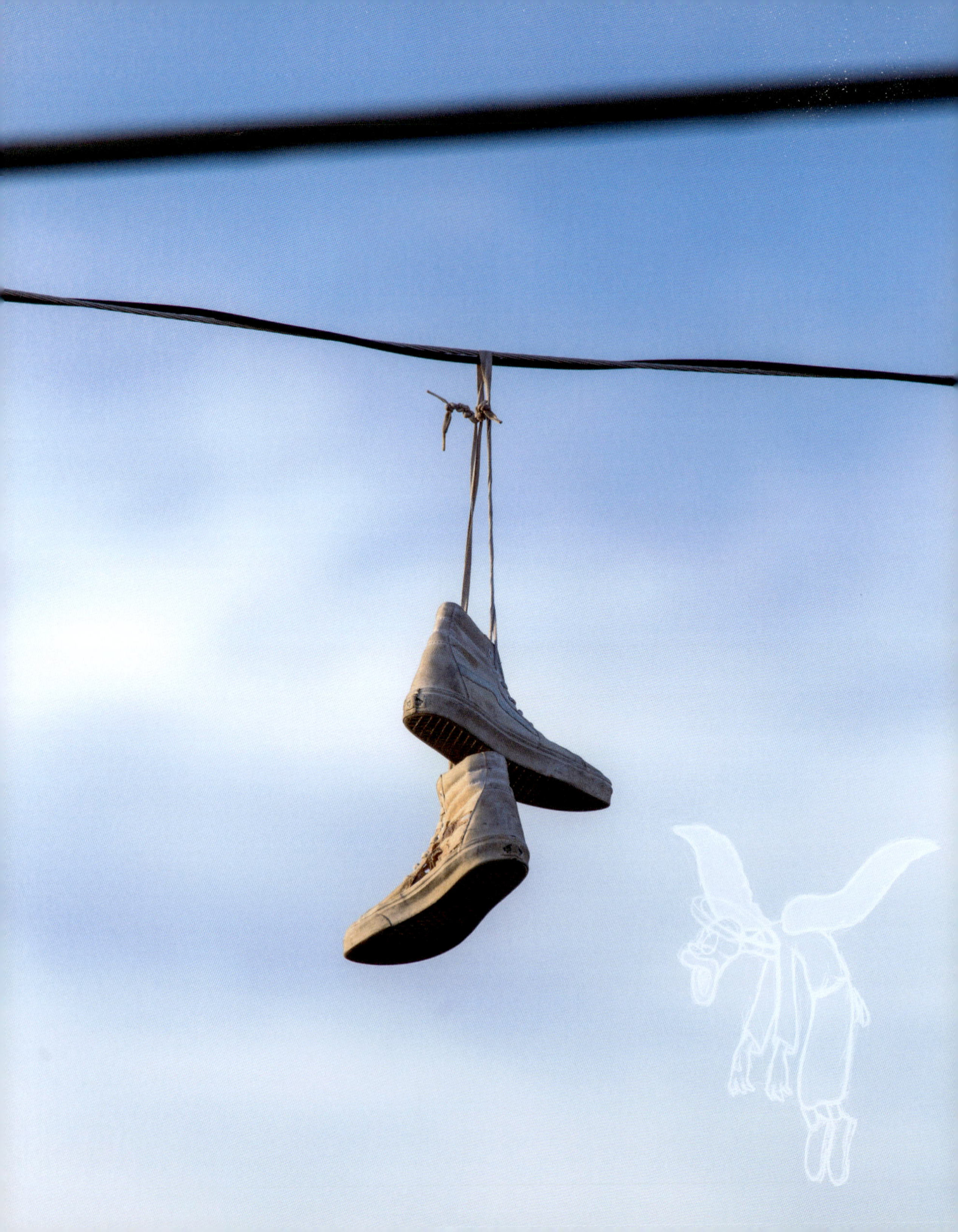

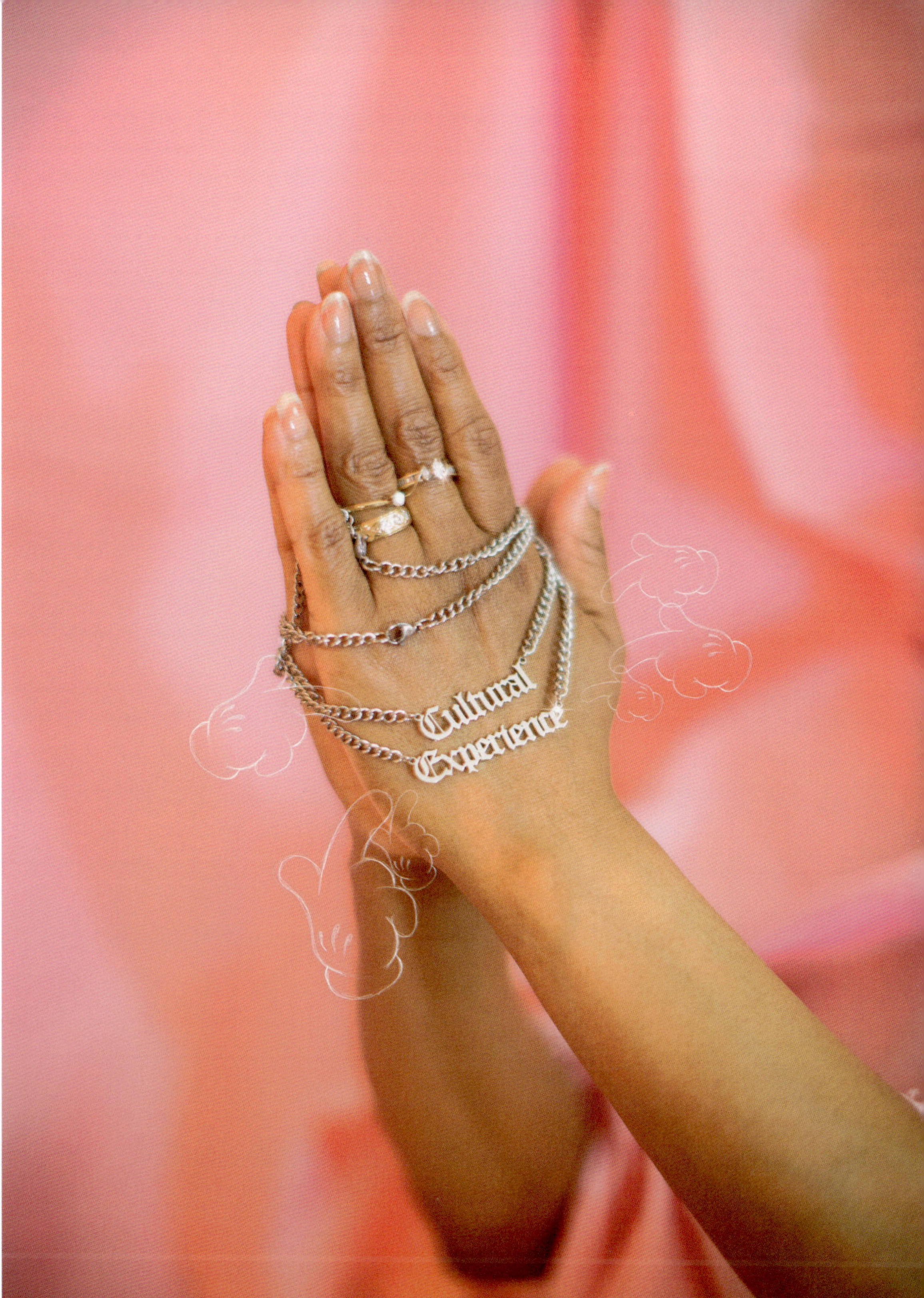
Cultural
Experience

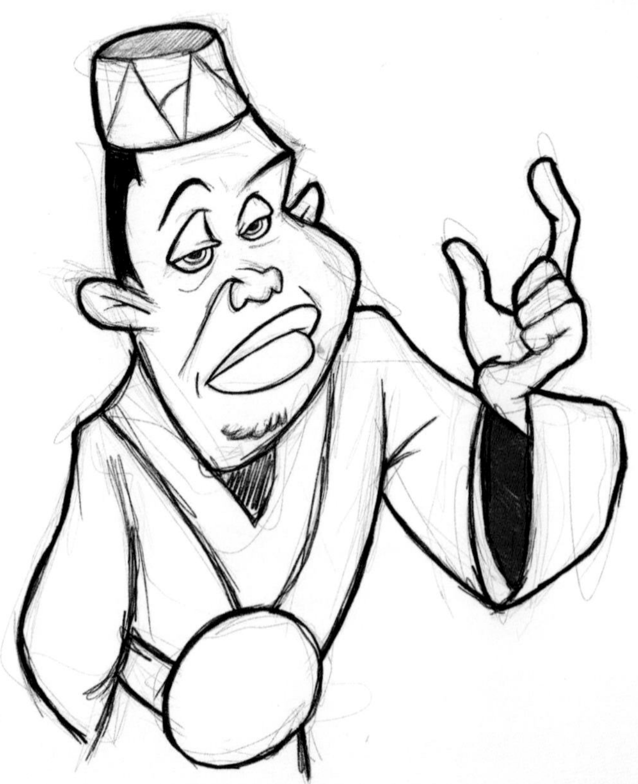

"THE SHORTEST MONTH OF THE YEAR"

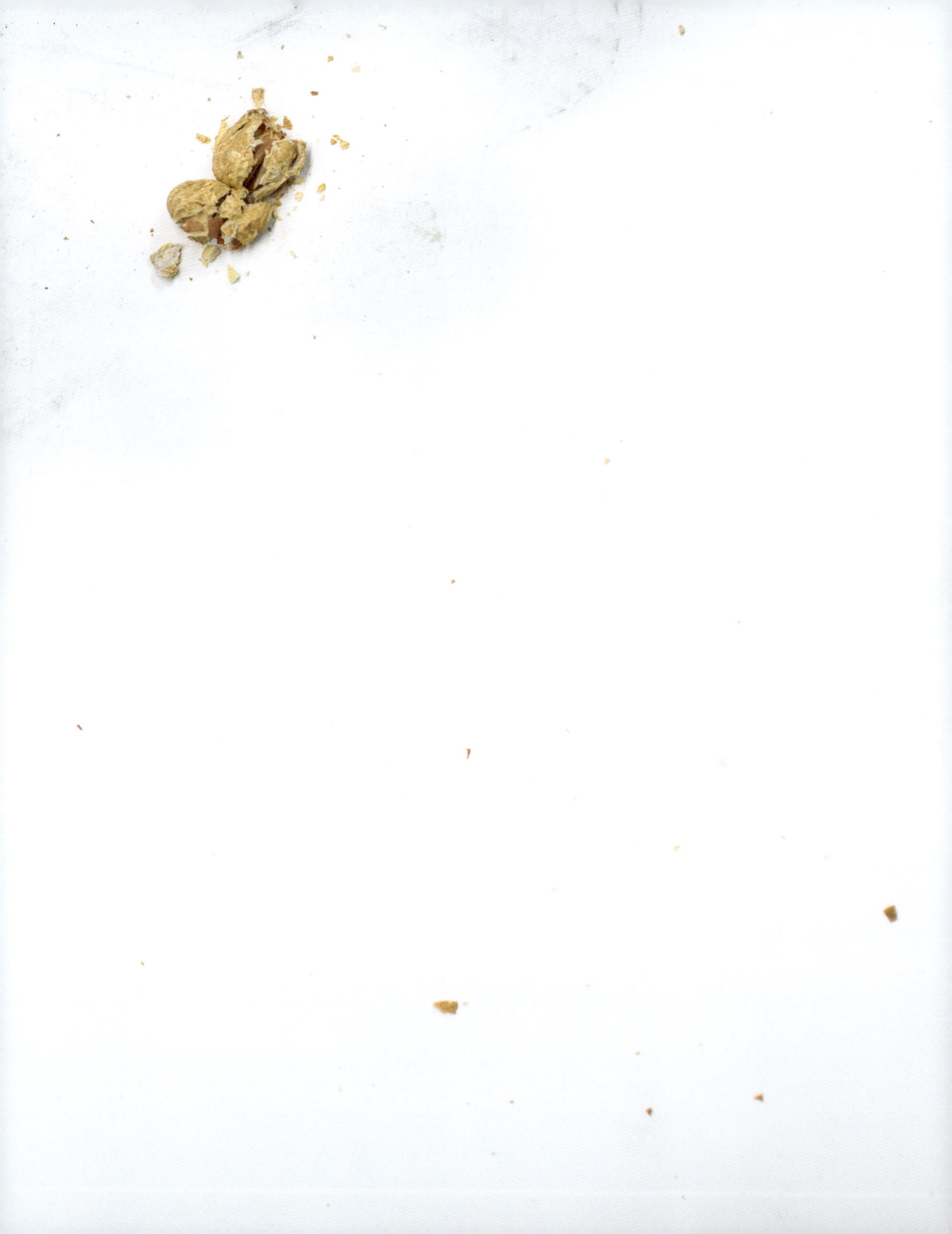

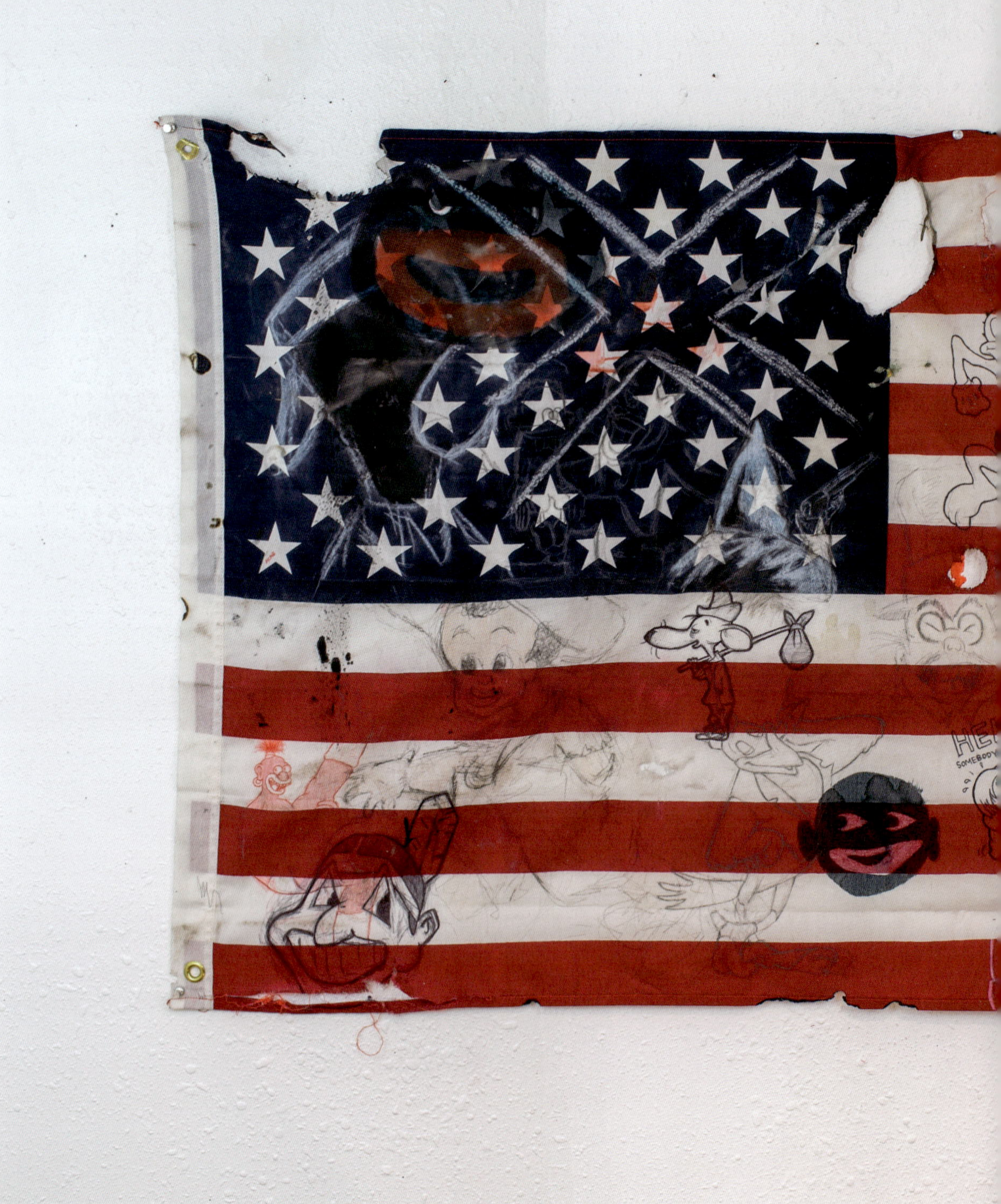
SOMEBODY

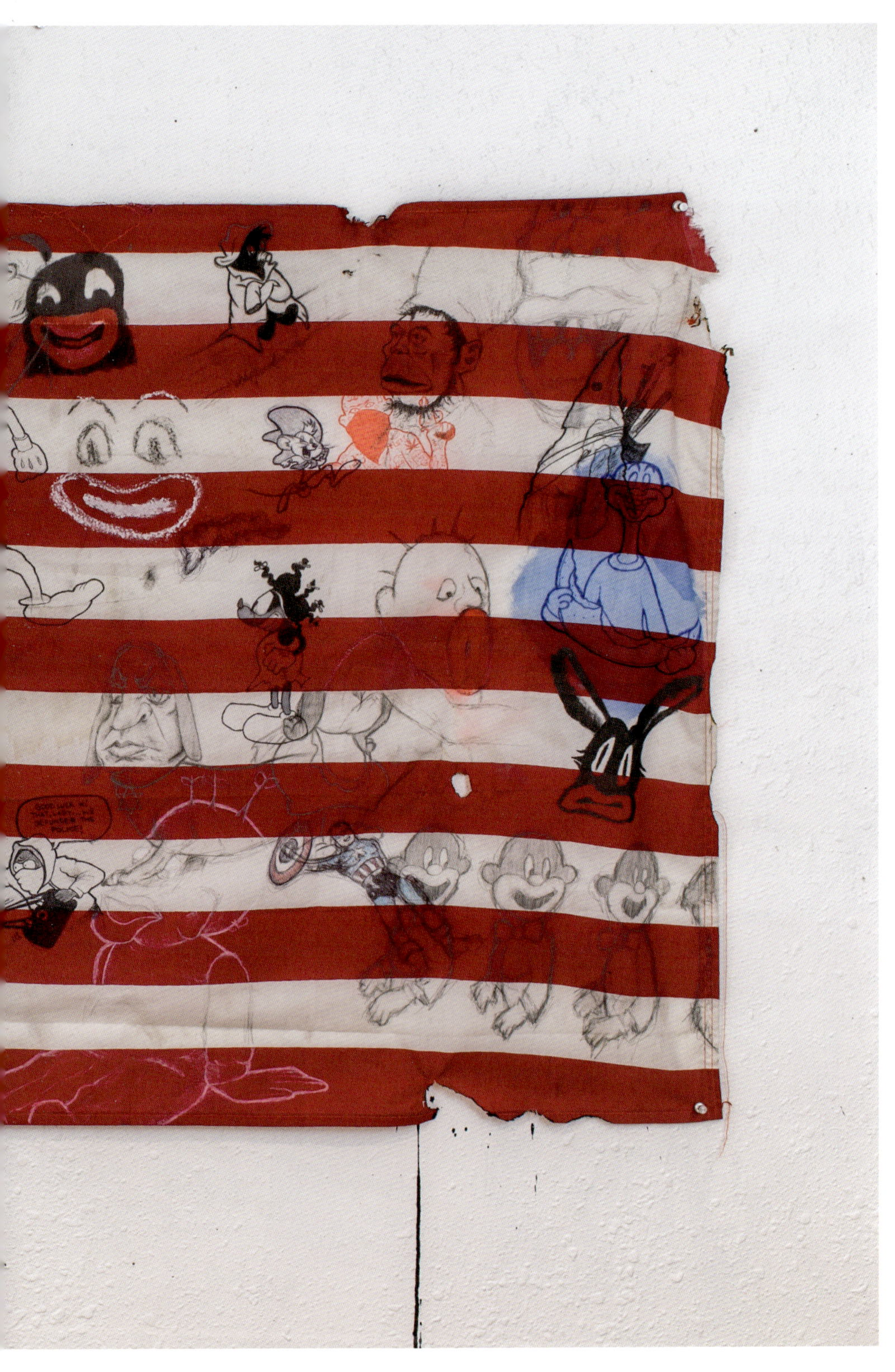

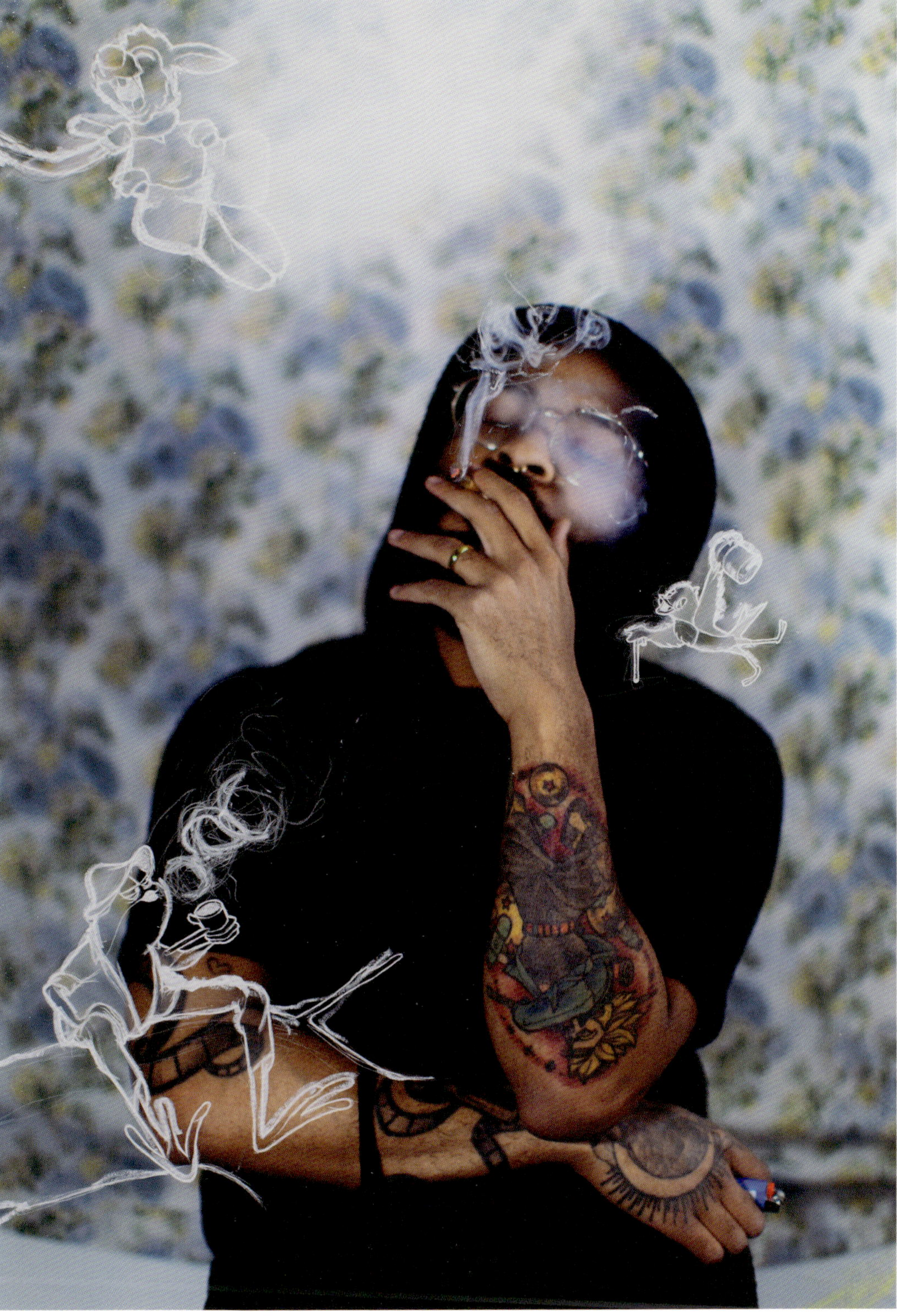